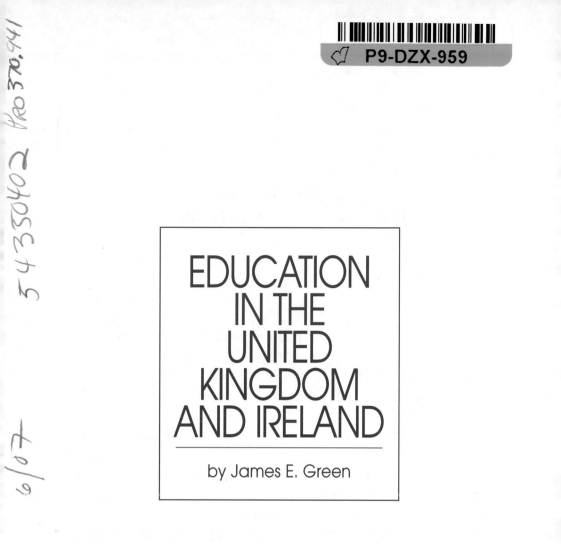

EDUCATION IN THE UNITED KINGDOM AND IRELAND

by James E. Green

Phi Delta Kappa
International Studies in Education

We can only see in a picture what our experience permits us to see.

Edgar Dale

The Phi Delta Kappa International Studies in Education Series was established as a way to enlarge the common experience of education by publishing studies that bring to readers knowledge of heretofore unfamiliar theories, philosophies, and practices in the profession of education.

As the interdependence of nations becomes increasingly evident and necessary with the passage of time, so too must our understandings about education become shared property. In this sharing, we come increasingly to comprehend one another across civilizations and cultures, for education is at the core of human endeavor. Through education we pass on to succeeding generations not merely the accumulated wisdom of our past but the vision and means to create the future.

Education in the United Kingdom and Ireland is the seventh monograph in this series.

Previous titles:
Elementary Teacher Education in Korea
Teacher Education in the People's Republic of China
Innovation in Russian Schools
Changing Traditions in Germany's Public Schools
German Higher Education: Issues and Challenges
French Elementary Education and the Ecole Moderne

INTERNATIONAL STUDIES IN EDUCATION

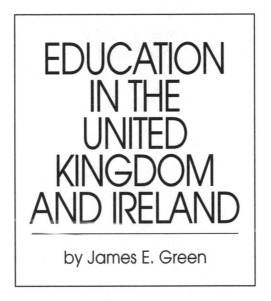

EDUCATION IN THE UNITED KINGDOM AND IRELAND

by James E. Green

PHI DELTA KAPPA
EDUCATIONAL FOUNDATION
Bloomington, Indiana
U.S.A.

Cover design by
Peg Caudell

Library of Congress Catalog Card Number 2001086004
ISBN 0-87367-832-X

TABLE OF CONTENTS

INTRODUCTION

Since the beginnings of U.S. public education, educators and critical observers have compared U.S. schools to those in other countries. Indeed, Gerald Gutek, in *American Education in a Global Society* (1993), observed that our U.S. public education system is the product of such comparisons. Horace Mann borrowed liberally from the Prussian school system when he established the common schools for Massachusetts. Earlier, Thomas Jefferson's proposal for Virginia's school system had clear connections to 18th century Europe.

Today we continue to compare our schools to those of other nations, though our motives for doing so seem to have changed. Recent comparative studies have been more intent on ranking the results than on actually reflecting on the systems and their intricacies. And too often the outcome has been merely an impetus for self-flagellation. *A Nation at Risk* (National Commission on Excellence in Education 1983) is a classic example of how international comparisons can be used to inflame a discussion on national education policy. More recently, the *Third International Mathematics and Science Study* provided an example of how studies rich in student achievement data will be given national attention more for the rankings of countries than for any insight into education systems either here or abroad (Atkin and Black 1997).

We may argue over the validity of some of the observations made in *A Nation at Risk*, *TIMSS*, or any of the numerous reports issued by the International Association for the Evaluation of Educational Achievement. And we might even question the political motivation of some of the conclusions. However, we can agree that international comparisons can stir a passion for change by causing us to more closely examine our own culture and its institutions. As Margaret Mead demonstrated convincingly throughout her career as a cultural anthropologist, we gain our most penetrating insights into our own social institutions when we examine the institutions of other countries.

Who is first? Who is last? Where do we rank? Too often these questions become both the purpose and extent of comparative studies. Regrettably, they miss the point entirely. In their place, we should ask more complex questions — questions that will lead us to a better understanding of the histories and cultures that form the context for schooling in a diverse *global* society. How are we similar? Where do we differ? What are the reasons for these similarities and differences? What can we learn from one another? These are the questions that, in the true spirit of Mead, we should ask when we examine the schools of other countries. When we earnestly seek answers to these questions, then the conclusions we draw are more likely to inform the improvement of our schools.

A "new order" of the world's economic environment has brought closer scrutiny of American schools and, consequently, a renewed interest in comparative education studies. Whereas Thomas Jefferson and Horace Mann looked to Europe for ideas as they were designing new systems of public education, recent international comparisons have been used more as a basis for critiquing school performance.

A couple of changes in the nature of global commerce account for much of the revived interest in international comparisons. First, about two decades ago the rising prominence of Japan and the leading nations of the European Union as global economic powers began to challenge America's position as the world's economic engine. Second, the essential nature of the global economy changed from independence to interdependence. During this same brief span of two decades, the norms for evaluating American pupils changed from national to international in scope. Gerald Gutek (1993) observed that the connection between the globalization of commerce and the renewed interest in comparing American schools internationally is more than coincidental.

Readers may recall that in the years immediately following World War II, the American economy thrived and Americans boasted of their supremacy as an economic power. In the perception of many, not just at home but also abroad, the United States was the world's leader in almost every way imaginable. And so, even while critics leveled some legitimate charges against American education, few policy changes resulted. In fact, education change was on the back burner in public policy discussion — that is, until the Soviet Union launched Sputnik in 1957. Suddenly the focus changed, and education was in the spotlight. Fear that the Soviet education system was superior to that of the United States and that the balance of power would tip in the direction of the Eastern Bloc during this Cold War era stimulated the U.S. Congress to pour money for science and mathematics education into the public schools. Even so, disenchantment with American education was not so widespread that "education reform" had become part of every political candidate's agenda. That would not happen for several more years. Instead, in the 1960s the American economy continued to prosper and other points of tension, such as the civil rights movement and deepening involvement in Vietnam, dominated public debate.

However, in the 1970s a combination of international events began a broader erosion of American public confidence in many of their institutions, and much of that erosion can be traced to the state of the economy. The oil embargo by OPEC and the emergence of Japan and the European Union as world economic powers came as stark evidence that the United States could no longer take its dominance in world commerce for granted.

During the same decade, public schools were buffeted by a host of problems, ranging from heightened awareness of drugs and crime to student social protests. A legal environment that diminished the authority of school officials and mandates to expand education opportunities converged at the same time that urban decay was reaching the point of despair in many cities. And all these were in the air just as societal expectations for schools were rising. As Berliner and Biddle observed in *The Manufac-*

3

tured Crisis: Myths, Fraud, and the Attack on American Public Schools (1997), the public grew disenchanted about education during the 1970s. Such public anxiety, combined with the economic pressure from overseas, became fertile ground for a new generation of critics.

The mounting national doubt about its education system was expressed in *A Nation at Risk* in 1983. A major premise of the document was that American schools were inferior to those in other nations, and the American quality of life was threatened by the decline of its education system. Numerous comparisons were cited, typified by the following:

> International comparisons of student achievement . . . reveal that on 19 academic tests American students were never first or second and . . . were last seven times. (p. 8)

Such statements became an impetus for the most recent wave of school reform. Political candidates were handed a risk-free cause to champion, therefore public debate on strategies for education reform became highly politicized. That was the more negative consequence. But on a positive note, researchers began to revisit the data from international comparisons, and finding a cultural context for interpreting the data became significant. Comparative education regained an important place in education dialogue.

Comparative education serves many purposes, but two stand out for educators striving to improve school systems. Foremost is advancing the understanding of one's own system of education. In a 1988 survey, scholars in the field agreed that a primary objective of comparative education is to gain insight into one's own system (Ross et al. 1992). Students of a second language often have observed that it was not until they learned the grammar of a foreign language that they began to comprehend the grammar of their own language. The same applies to the study of social institutions; comparisons provide a cognitive map and a contextual framework to help in our understanding. Moreover, comparisons of education systems have a utilitarian purpose.

4

They help us find solutions to our own education problems. Indeed, when asked to rank the objectives of comparative education, researchers stated that the most important was "to search for lessons that can be deduced from the variations in educational practice in different societies" (Ross et al. 1992, p. 115). Thomas Jefferson and Horace Mann were right.

However, the lens of comparative study of education systems can be clouded by cross-cultural differences. Recent and much-publicized attempts to compare pupil achievement data between cultures provide numerous examples (Atkin and Black 1997). Schools operate within a cultural context defined by political, religious, and philosophical beliefs. To compare a social institution that is the product of one culture to one that is the product of another is like comparing the differences in the weather from one place to another. We can observe the differences. We also can observe how people acclimate to those differences. We might even be inclined to express our personal preferences about weather. But we cannot make a value judgment about one weather system being "better" than another. One might be good for producing grain, another might be good for producing fruit. But both are suitable for agriculture.

When we study education systems through the lens of comparison, we are observing different systems engaged in the same enterprise. We begin the comparison by observing the cultural similarities and differences, then we move to the distinctions we can make between the social institutions. Only to the extent that the differences between the institutions exist within the same social milieu can we observe whether they are significant for comparative purposes. Moreover, only to the extent that we can observe that practices within a particular education system are compatible with the social values and belief systems of another can we begin to discuss importing or exporting those practices.

Comparisons require points of reference. In comparative education there is no prescribed paradigm. Indeed, many scholars in the field argue that there is no prescribed method. A presenter at the 1979 annual conference of the Comparative International

Education Society succinctly stated the current methodological position for comparative education studies:

> someone said that there is no comparative method, just comparative data. If this is so, there is no constraint on theoretical perspective or research methods. (Cited in Ross et al. 1992, p. 118)

In comparative education, as in any of the social sciences, points of reference and methods of inquiry must be tailored to fit the particular problem.

In this overview of the education systems in the United Kingdom and Ireland, my purpose is to describe the national systems and to identify those practices that are noticeably different from the education system in the United States. Even though similarities in the cultures — English, Welsh, Scottish, Irish, and American — are prevalent, specific points of reference are needed for the descriptions to be useful for comparative purposes. Accordingly, this overview is organized into two principal divisions: First, the social foundations of a nation's education system and, second, the curriculum and its implementation in the schools.

The social foundations include a sketch of each nation's society, with particular attention to social conditions and trends that affect the schooling of children. I also provide a survey of the history of a nation's education system, with emphasis on the record of education reform. Next, the social context for describing the education systems of England and Ireland includes an explanation of the levels of governmental control. In the case of education in England and Wales, I separate these divisions into two chapters. The two divisions are combined into single chapters for the other countries.

As educators of any nation know, a system for formal education can be understood only when the life of students and teachers is well described. The content of the curriculum and how it is assessed, how teachers teach, school culture and its effect on children, the quality of professional life for teachers — these are all subjects that are required for any real understanding of an education system. Thus each overview of these education systems also addresses curricula, programs for assessment, and the status of the teacher.

The education systems of the United Kingdom and the Republic of Ireland are of particular interest to American educators because they share a heritage and language with the United States. They also deal with many of the same social problems and economic imperatives. Of course, the three systems — the United Kingdom, Ireland, and the United States — also are quite different from one another. Indeed, the fascination of a comparative study focusing on the United Kingdom, Ireland, and the United States lies in how nations and states can be so similar and yet so different. By exploring differences in policies and practices, given the cultural similarities and intersecting histories, we gain a better understanding of our own education system. Furthermore, we may even begin to seriously question some of our own assumptions as we strive to improve our nation's schools.

In Chapters 1 through 4, I describe the education systems in England and Wales, Scotland, and Northern Ireland. I am indebted to Sheryl O'Sullivan for writing Chapter 5 about the Republic of Ireland. Then, in Chapter 6, I synthesize these descriptions around the issues that charge the debates on education policy in the United States. The following questions serve as the outline for the concluding comparisons:

- What is the agenda for education reform?
- What are the goals for the curriculum? How are these goals assessed?
- How does the education system foster community in a diverse society?
- What teaching methods are prevalent?
- What is the professional status of teachers? How are they prepared?

Examining these questions from the perspectives of the British and Irish should prove helpful to American educators who are looking for new ideas to help inform discussions of education policy in the United States.

CHAPTER ONE

SCHOOLS IN ENGLAND AND WALES: SOCIAL, HISTORICAL, AND POLITICAL CONTEXTS

The English education system is like its history, a paradox that conspires against any simple explanation. While English education has been the subject of admiration by educators around the world, it also has been the focus of severe criticism from within its own society. Yet the English staunchly defend the system from any criticism that originates outside their borders. Where one expects to find centrality of purpose, there is diversity of opinion. Where one might hope to find diversity, there is a devotion to things and ideas that are steadfastly "British." Education governance is both centralized and decentralized, and the national curriculum is progressive and traditional at the same time.

Understanding the system of English education requires an examination from many perspectives, and always it requires grounding those observations in the context of today's society. Thus I would begin this two-part examination of English education with a description of the population that composes its school communities. A brief historical sketch is necessary background for understanding today's currents of education reform, as well as the several models for government control of schools in England. Finally, I describe the various patterns of grade-level organization for primary and secondary schools.

Social Contexts

Schools are a social institution. Therefore the first step to understanding the system for England and Wales is to view the population it serves. Of special importance is the degree to which the various descriptors of society are in a state of change, and especially noteworthy is the increasing diversity that characterizes much of contemporary English culture. In general, England and Wales both are densely populated, each having a large, vital, middle class. While ethnic diversity is increasing, the population and the predominant culture remain overwhelming white and overwhelmingly *British*, with all the connotations of that descriptor.

The British. As difficult as it might be to describe a people as contradictory as the British, an attempt at characterization is helpful before delving into the details of one of its social institutions. First, for a land as geographically compact as England, it is a place of remarkable variety. On a single day's journey by train, a traveler can marvel at the pastoral lakes of Cumbria, the austere moors of Yorkshire, the rugged mountains of Wales, and the luster of white coastal cliffs near Dover. This one-day journey would pass through the quaint country villages of the Cotswolds and the great industrial and commercial centers of Manchester and Birmingham. And the excursion would include London, which remains one of the world's foremost cultural centers. In the same field of vision, the traveler might see genteel pastures of grazing sheep set against a backdrop of bleak factories reminiscent of scenes from a Dickens novel. No wonder the people are so diverse, and no wonder they combine a sense of what is graceful with hard-nosed practicality.

On this island the people speak a common language but with accents as varied as those found on the North American continent. And they hold to their regional identities with tenacity. Indeed, the Welsh and the Scots are so insistent on maintaining their cultural heritages that special legal systems and education institutions have evolved. Because of these differences, as well as the influences of rapidly increasing populations from diverse cultures, a composite character sketch of the national ethos is nearly impossible. Or it would be at least as difficult as any similar attempt in the United States. Nonetheless, a British stereotype persists.

A popular guidebook depicts the British as reserved, even aloof, with a natural preference for understatement. The British describe themselves as having a gift for compromise (Locke, Cavendish, and Rogerson 1996). (Although this latter point is hardly noticed by historians of British colonialism.) Stereotypical "Brits" also have a sense of humor that leans toward irony. They are not reluctant to poke fun at themselves or their fellow countrymen. However, the foreigner who tries the same joke had better be wary because that supposedly ironic sense of humor turns to bulldog ferocity if national pride is chaffed in any way.

The British also can be described as resisting change. While aspects of the society can be as modern as any in the world in terms of technology and lifestyle, that change has not been homogenized into British culture. "Marbleized" change might be a more accurate description, explaining why a franchised fast-food restaurant can be seen coexisting beside a quintessential pub, or a supermarket can be found across the street from a traditional cheesemonger. "Marbleized" change also aptly describes the social fabric of Britain, and it certainly describes recent developments in the education system.

Demography. According to a report in 1991 by the Office of Population Census and Surveys (OPCS), the United Kingdom's population numbers more than 55 million in a geographic area barely the size of Oregon. The people of England and Wales account for approximately 90% of that number.

England is divided into eight geographic regions for census-reporting purposes. These eight regions include a population of more than 46 million. Of these, the southeast region, which includes London, is the most populous. It accounts for more than a third of the population, and the other seven regions range individually from about 13% to about 4% of the total population. Wales has a population of fewer than three million, or about 5% of the total in the United Kingdom (OPCS 1991).

As in many economically developed nations, the population of England and Wales is aging. When the baby-boom generation

11

completed its formal education, the age structure of the population changed significantly. In 1971 approximately one-quarter of the population was school age, but now that proportion is slightly less than 20% (OPCS 1993*a*).

Family. The family structure has changed as much in Britain as it has in other nations of the Western world. Families are smaller. There are more births outside of marriage. And more homes are affected by divorce. As a consequence, single-parent families and merged families are more common, and the "traditional" family is rapidly becoming the nontraditional family. The Central Statistical Office (CSO) reported in 1994 that the divorce rate has increased approximately by a multiple of four since 1951, and the rate of children born outside of marriage is six times higher now. Today about one-third of all births are out of wedlock (CSO 1994*b*).

The role of the mother also has changed in the past several decades. Today nearly half of the workforce is female, though nearly half of the women working are employed part time (OPCS 1992*a*; CSO 1994*b*). Most mothers now work outside the home at least part time.

Social classes. British social scientists use occupation as the means for determining social class (Mackinnon et al. 1995). The Office of Population Censuses and Surveys has designated five categories for defining social class, each of which is based on occupation. The five categories include the following, with approximate percentages for each shown in parentheses (OPCS 1992*b*):

Professional (6%)
Managerial and technical (27%)
Skilled, non-manual (24%)
Skilled, manual (23%)
Partly skilled (15%)
Unskilled (6%)

According to these statistics, about half the population is considered middle class, with the distribution slightly skewed toward the upper middle class. However, statistics describing social class do not tell the whole story. Mackinnon, Stratham, and Hales (1995) observed that other telling statistics, such as the increasing frequency of births among the lower class and the increasing frequency of single-parent families, describe a higher proportion of children of poverty attending schools than the OPCS statistics would suggest.

Ethnic groups. All of the various atypical ethnic groups together include less than one-tenth of the total population. Moreover, almost half of all nonwhite residents of the island live in the greater London area (OPCS 1993*b*). This disparity is more prevalent when comparing certain boroughs of London with some of the rural counties. For example, Teague (1993, cited in Mackinnon et al. 1995) reported that in the London boroughs of Brent or Ealing, approximately half the population is nonwhite; however, in the rural counties of Berwickshire or Sutherland, less than 1% is nonwhite.

Ethnic diversity influences economic characteristics as well. Whereas 20% of the white population is classified as "semiskilled" or "unskilled manual" in terms of social class, some 30% of the Pakistani or Bangladeshi immigrant population, for example, is so classified. In another example of ethnic difference, when the top two social classes are analyzed by ethnic group, 22% of the white population is considered "professional" or "employers/managers" compared to only 11% of individuals whose origins are the West Indies (OPCS 1992*b*).

According to a 1994 report by the Central Statistical Office, demographic characteristics for the family also differ by ethnic group. The average white family has slightly fewer than two children per household, for example, whereas the average Pakistani or Bangladeshi family has slightly more than three. In another example, more than half of all single mothers are West Indian, compared to only 11% who are white (CSO 1994*b*).

Perhaps most significant in its bearing on schools is the fact that the nonwhite population is significantly younger than the white population. About one-third of nonwhites are school age, compared to only one-fifth of whites (Mackinnon et al. 1995).

Education History in Brief

The development of elementary and secondary schools in England and Wales was haphazard until the early 20th century. Parliament gave little, if any, attention to education policy. Schools simply evolved. Part of the government's neglect can be attributed to the social class-consciousness that is evident in all aspects of British culture even today. In brief, children of the aristocracy and the professional class attended privately endowed schools, which paradoxically were called "public" through the mid-20th century. Middle-class children typically attended schools operated by churches, guilds, or private schoolmasters. And working-class children, if they attended schools at all, received their formal education through voluntary schools operated by religious organizations or charitable institutions. Not until the latter part of the 19th century was there any serious attempt to provide for government regulation or systematic state support. Education was viewed as a privilege, and consequently the system (rather, the lack of a system) contributed to the social status quo. This laissez faire policy resulted in the nation relying exclusively on the "public" schools for the education of its leaders.

As the 19th century drew to a close, significant change began to occur in the role that government played in schooling the nation's children. Indeed, the Elementary Education Act of 1870, also know as the Forster Act, marked the beginning of the modern era of British education (Mackinnon et al. 1995). The Forster Act divided the country into school districts and made provisions for local school boards to levy taxes to support schools for areas in which none existed. These "board schools," as they were called, were nondenominational and subject to the oversight of the education board that supported them. Even with these sweeping improvements, however, there were neither general curriculum guidelines nor requirements for teachers. Schools also could still assess fees, which meant that many children simply did not attend because their parents could not afford to send them. Not until 1891 was an elementary education made free by act of Parliament. And it was not until 1902 that Parliament passed an act creating a system of secondary education (Mackinnon et al. 1995).

Acts of Parliament. Since the Forster Act of 1870, Parliament has passed more than 50 acts affecting education in England and Wales, and the number swells to 75 if Northern Ireland and Scotland are included (Mackinnon et al. 1995). Close examination of these acts reveals that the modern history of education in England and Wales is one of oscillating power between the Conservative and Labour political parties. Especially evident is the emergence in the 20th century of the Labour Party's agenda for social reform, followed by the reemergence of the Conservative Party in the 1980s and its program for radical reform of state-supported education.

Several acts of Parliament stand out as watershed events. While the Forster Act created a loosely knitted system for elementary schools in 1870, it was not until more than 20 years later, with the Education Act of 1891, that an elementary education became free — and even then parents were responsible for the payment of incidental fees. Finally, with the passage of the Fisher Act in 1918, all fees were abolished and an elementary education became truly accessible to all children. However, secondary education remained available until the mid-20th century only to those who could afford to pay for it. In 1944 the Butler Act was passed, and free compulsory education was extended through age 15 (Mackinnon et al. 1995).

The Butler Act of 1944 was an extraordinary development in education policy for England and Wales. Having successfully faced the challenge of a full-fledged foreign assault during World War II, the nation was hardly in the mood merely to tweak the system when it came to social policy. The British mentality was one of action at the close of the war, and education became another front. The Butler Act marks the beginning of a truly national

15

system for education. In addition to mandating free compulsory education through age 15, it restructured the national administration of schools. The old Board of Education was elevated in importance and renamed the Ministry of Education, and the education minister was given a proactive leadership role for the nation's schools. The act also expanded the concept of government-supported education to include preschool and community-based education and recreation, as well as allowing local education authorities to provide a wide array of support services to the children of the community. Thus nutrition and health care became part of the mission of state-supported education (Mackinnon et al. 1995).

A generation later Parliament passed the Education Act of 1980 (Mackinnon et al. 1995). While not nearly as radical as the Butler Act of 1944, this act introduced several new concepts in public education policy. First, the act declared that parents had the right to choose which school their children would attend. While parent choice of schools still rages as a politically controversial issue in the United States, Parliament decisively resolved the question as soon as parents began to grow disenchanted with the increasing bureaucracy of the education system. In addition, Parliament responded to an increasingly powerful movement in Wales for more recognition of the unique cultural character of that region. In particular, the chief education officer in Wales was authorized to fund bilingual education — English and Welsh — for elementary and secondary schools in Wales.

During the 1980s the rise of conservatism in British politics was especially evident in education policy. In 1984 the Education Grants and Award Acts, in effect, curtailed the discretion that local education authorities had in spending funds received from the national government (Mackinnon et al. 1995). This act proved to be a harbinger of a power shift from local education authorities to the national government that came with the Education Reform Act of 1988.

Two provisions of the Education Reform Act of 1988 stand out, and both serve as examples of the centralizing of authority for education that education reformers advocated as necessary. First, a national curriculum was instituted when Parliament created the National Curriculum Council for England and the Curriculum Council for Wales. Prior to this era of reform, Parliament merely insisted that local education authorities provide education for their respective communities; now it prescribed in specific terms the kind of education. Also, the act set up a system of "grant-maintained schools" to complement the existing system of "maintained schools." The result of this action was a provision for local governing bodies, with the consent of the majority of parents, to secede from the local education authority and receive funding from the national government directly. Highly controversial when they were implemented by the Education Reform Act of 1988, grant-maintained schools were seen by the anti-education establishment as necessary to dislodge local education authorities that had become resistant to change. The educators in the local education authorities saw the creation of grant-maintained schools as yet another encroachment by the national government (Mackinnon et al. 1995).

Widespread disenchantment with local education authorities was at the root of many of the changes in the Education Reform Act of 1988. Discontent also was at the heart of another controversial feature of the act: Tenure was abolished for faculty in universities, though the act provided that faculty could not be dismissed on ideological grounds alone. Without question, 1988 was a year in which the academic ground shook in Great Britain.

Official reports. During the second half of the 20th century more than 50 reports were commissioned by various government ministries. In many cases these reports were instrumental to the development of education policy in England and Wales. However, when official government reports average approximately one per year, we must be skeptical of their real effect at the level where teaching and learning occurs. Close examination reveals that there were many more recommendations than actual changes during these 50 years. Nevertheless, a survey of these reports provides an overview of the shifting attitudes that form public policy in education.

During the 19th century and the first half of the 20th century, the education system was a mirror of social class-consciousness. Following World War II, however, a social reform movement began to assert itself in many quarters of English life. Government reports on education policy serve as examples. In 1944 the Fleming Report was published. This report represented a concentrated effort to integrate the "public" schools into the state-supported education system. Specifically, the report proposed a system of government grants to students who attended these private, independent schools. While the recommendations for greater participation by the public schools in the state-supported education system was well received, it was never implemented because of the unwillingness of either the national government or the local education authorities to fund the grants. Still, the report demonstrated a desire on the part of education policy makers to begin breaking down the social-class divisions so apparent in English society (Mackinnon et al. 1995).

Three years later, in 1947, the Central Advisory Council for Education (CACE) published the Clark Report. The Clark Report took a comprehensive look at the needs of the education system, especially the transition between school and work; and it proposed greatly enhanced support at all levels (Mackinnon et al. 1995). In effect, the Clark Report began to assess the changes that had begun to take place following the Butler Act of 1944, and its recommendations were for the purpose of focusing and refining the sweeping policy changes that had been implemented just a few years before.

The Gurney-Dixon Report of 1954 was the first comprehensive evaluation of the changes in education policy that were instituted by the Butler Act. While generally supportive of the initiatives taken 10 years previously, the authors of the report observed that very little progress had been made in reducing social-class inequities in the education system. Its recommendations called for greater effort at achieving the principle of equal education opportunity that was espoused in the Butler Act (Mackinnon et al. 1995).

In the late 1950s and early 1960s the movement toward expanding education opportunity continued with the publication of three reports by the Central Advisory Councils on Education: the Crowther Report of 1959, the Newsome Report of 1963, and the Robbins Report of 1963-64. The cumulative effect of these reports was to raise the school leaving age to 16, generally upgrade facilities, and improve curriculum. In particular, the Robbins Report made a strong case for higher education access becoming an important strategy for improving the quality of life for the working class (Mackinnon et al. 1995).

What the Crowther, Newsome, and Robbins reports did to raise the level of public awareness for secondary and higher education, the Plowden Report of 1967 did for primary education (Mackinnon et al. 1995). Unfortunately, raising the level of public awareness does not always result in decisive action by Parliament, and many of the Plowden Report's more practical recommendations languished. Nonetheless, the Plowden Report must be given credit for creating an agenda for improvement that would surface in various acts of Parliament 10 years later.

During the 1970s the professional preparation of teachers received increasing attention. Colleges of education affiliated with other "further education" institutions, such as polytechnic colleges; and the professional training of teachers was integrated into general higher education. Most of these changes occurred as a result of the James Report of 1972, which is credited with providing a framework for teacher education that continues to this day (Mackinnon et al. 1995).

During the late 1970s and early 1980s concern for social reform dominated education policy debates, and numerous reports resulted. Two have historic significance. In 1978 the Warnock Report recommended important changes in education policy for students with special needs. Indeed, it was the impetus for the Education Act of 1981, which was landmark legislation with regard to special education. In 1985 the Swan Report gave careful scrutiny to the underachievement of children from minority populations, and initiatives for multicultural education were introduced. Both reports — Warnock and Swan — were instrumental in continuing an agenda of social reform through education (Mackinnon et al. 1995).

Education reform became a worldwide movement during the 1980s and 1990s, and Great Britain was among the first to join the parade. Two reports in particular were important influences on education policy for England and Wales. The 1987 Report of the National Curriculum Task Group (the "Black Report") was a precursor to the Education Reform Act of 1988, which officially nationalized the curriculum. The Dearing Report of 1993 further developed the scope of the national curriculum and its system for assessment. More prescriptive goals for instruction and a more elaborate model for assessment resulted from these reports (Mackinnon et al. 1995).

In summary, it can be said that English schools developed through two distinct eras, one private, one public (in the American, rather than the British, sense). As Gutek (1993) observed, the first era was marked by a laissez faire policy on the government's part. Private schools served the aristocracy and, where they were available, volunteer, philanthropic schools served the working class. Of course, the charitable schools were few in number; therefore, the influence of graduates from the elite private schools has been enormous throughout the history of Great Britain.

"Public" schools, the most prestigious of the private schools, have been characterized as models for secondary education for centuries. According to Gutek (1993), nine are most frequently mentioned among the elite: Charterhouse, Eton, Harrow, Merchant Taylor's, Rugby, St. Paul's, Shrewsbury, Winchester, and Westminster. Winchester was founded in 1342 as a preparatory school for Oxford. The others similarly have defined their purpose as securing the admission and success of graduates in the top tier of British higher education, namely Cambridge or Oxford. Education elitism remains the hallmark of the public school tradition even today.

At the other end of the continuum, education opportunities were limited for working-class children in this era. The "system" consisted of a miscellany of parish schools, dame schools, privately endowed orphanages, and private entrepreneurial efforts. Education, when it was available, was woefully inadequate in comparison to the "public" schools. Dissatisfaction with the obvious limitations of these disjointed efforts led to widespread attempts of reform.

The public era — that is, the emergence of a national system of education for all — began in the mid-19th century with the rise of political liberalism and resulting social reform legislation (Gutek 1993). William Gladstone, who became prime minister in 1868, was instrumental in the passage of the Forster Act. And from mid-century onward the competing political agendas of the Labour and Conservative parties formed and reformed the character of that national system. In the past two decades, education reform of schools in England and Wales has been driven by the same factors influencing education reform worldwide: the emergence of information technologies and the globalization of commerce.

Organization and Control

Primary and secondary education are the main divisions of what now constitutes compulsory public education in England and Wales. However, secondary education has numerous strands and levels that will befuddle a foreign observer on first examination. Postsecondary education also includes a wide range of options, some connecting to secondary education; in fact, some begin for students at age 16 and others begin following a two-year course of study that, for most students, occurs at age 18.

The system of state regulation likewise has many variations. Because the emergence of a national education system in England and Wales was the result of piecemeal legislation spanning a century or more, the nation has multiple structures for governing schools. Local boards control some. Others are accountable directly to the national Department for Education (DFE). In addition, the relationship between independent schools and state-supported schools is blurred by the policy of allowing government grants to enroll students.

Patterns for schooling. To understand best how control of schools is effected, it is necessary, first, to understand how the schools are organized. Some nine million students attend about 34,000 schools in the United Kingdom (England, Wales, Scotland, and Northern Ireland). School attendance is compulsory for children age five through 16, the primary and secondary levels; and it is optional for children younger than age five, which is the preschool level (Mackinnon et al. 1995).

Local education authorities (LEAs) are not required to provide state-supported preschools to children under the age of five, though many do. Approximately 69% of the three- and four-year-olds in Wales and 53% of the three- and four-year-olds in England attend state-maintained nursery schools or special nursery classes housed in the primary schools. The level of participation and the kinds of preschool available vary widely among the LEAs. In the northern counties the percentage of three- and four-year-olds enrolled in nursery classes runs as high as 75%, whereas in the southwestern counties the level averages 30%. There are more than a thousand state-maintained nursery schools, but the vast majority of preschool children attend nursery classes (sometimes called "reception" classes) in the primary schools. In addition, some children attend independent preschools, many of which are found in those areas where the LEAs do not provide for state-maintained early childhood education. While these independent nursery schools are regulated by local social services departments, their enrollments are not counted in the LEAs preschool enrollments. Therefore the number of children involved in early childhood education is even higher than the approximately 750,000 reported by the Department for Education. High standards for safety and education programming are required, with all teachers and assistants having received their training in programs approved by the National Nursery Examination Board (NNEB) (Mackinnon et al. 1995).

All children must attend school after they turn five, with primary schools providing education for children ages five through 11. Approximately 24,000 state-maintained primary schools are in operation, enrolling more than 4,700,000 pupils and employing more than 223,000 teachers (Mackinnon et al. 1995). Primary schools come in three varieties: *infant schools*, which are organized for pupils five through seven; *junior schools*, which are for pupils seven through 11; and combined infant and junior schools, which provide classes for pupils for the entire span of primary education (Gutek 1993). In recent years, the last type has become the most prevalent. Primary schools typically are small, most having fewer than 200 pupils. As a consequence, primary schools in England and Wales have retained a "neighborhood school" feel. With rare exceptions, children can walk to their primary school.

In recent years, the middle school has emerged in England, though the age range of children in middle schools varies widely. A middle school enrolling children eight through 12 years of age usually is classified as a primary school, whereas a middle school for children 10 through 14 is considered a secondary school. Some middle schools enroll children nine through 13, and they might be classified as either primary or secondary, depending on the local education authority's preference. Obviously, the development of the middle school concept in England has preceded the Department for Education's mechanism for labeling school organization types.

Nearly all of the middle schools in the United Kingdom are found in England. Wales has only one local education authority that offers a middle school, and Scotland has none (Mackinnon et al. 1995). Schools are smaller in Wales and Scotland, especially in the rural areas, and so the personal attention needed by students as they make the transition to secondary school happens naturally. Therefore middle schools may be seen as less needed.

Children in England and Wales must attend school until age 16, but most state-maintained secondary schools provide various education programs to age 19. About 4,700 state-maintained secondary schools enroll nearly 3.5 million pupils and employ about 233,000 teachers (Mackinnon et al. 1995).

The system for secondary education is comprised of two tracks: *grammar schools* for students seeking admission to a university and *secondary modern schools* for students who are not preparing for university admission. In the past two decades, these two tracks of schooling have been combined into the *comprehensive school*, wherein students have multiple options available to them and which students of all abilities may attend. From 1971 to 1991 the proportion of comprehensive schools increased from 36% to 84% (Mackinnon et al. 1995).

Secondary schools may include a *sixth form*, which refers to a program of study beyond the compulsory school attendance age. More than half of all comprehensive schools in England and Wales have the sixth form. Pupils in schools without a sixth form who wish to continue their education beyond the compulsory attendance age must attend a *sixth form college* (Mackinnon et al. 1995).

The Education Act of 1981, which followed the Warnock Report of 1978, provided for the education of children with special needs. As a result, the number of special schools has increased significantly in the past two decades. At present there are approximately 1,800 special schools serving 110,000 pupils with special needs. In addition, about 2,000 schools have special classes and units for children with special needs. In total, some 165,000 children are identified as requiring special education services — slightly less than 2% of the school population (Mackinnon et al. 1995).

Governance. An exception can be found to any generalization about the governance of schools in England and Wales. Even with the recent shift of control from local education authorities to the Department for Education, the governance of schools remains a system of partnerships between local and national government that varies from county to county (Mackinnon et al. 1995).

The central agency for education in England and Wales is the Department for Education, which is responsible for all state-maintained schools and certain aspects of independent schools. Separate agencies, the Further Education Funding Council and the Higher Education Funding Council, are organized within the Department for Education, and they are responsible for administering fiscal policy for postsecondary education. Another agency, the Office for Standards in Education, is independent of the Department for Education and is responsible for the inspection of schools (Mackinnon et al. 1995).

The role of the Office for Standards in Education (OFSTED) is similar to state accreditation. The agency is headed by Her Majesty's Chief Inspector of Schools, who oversees a staff of professionals who evaluate the condition of education being offered in the respective schools. Moreover, the scope of inspection is broad. According to the Department for Education, "Inspectors must report on the quality of education provided, the educational standards achieved, the efficiency of financial management and the 'spiritual, moral, social and cultural development' of pupils" (DFE 1993, p. 5, as cited in Mackinnon et al. 1995).

Wales has its own central agency, the Welsh Office Education Department. The Welsh Office Education Department is composed of four divisions: curriculum, administration, further and higher education, and culture and recreation. In addition, Wales has an agency responsible for school inspection that is separate from the Education Department. In effect, Wales operates its own system independent of England's Department for Education with the exception of policies for teachers, which remain with the English Department for Education. These separate agencies notwithstanding, the education systems in Wales and England are very similar; and many public policy statements are issued jointly by the two national agencies (Mackinnon et al. 1995).

The basic political entity for operating schools in England and Wales is the *local education agency* (LEA). England's 109 LEAs correspond to other political subdivisions — counties, metropolitan districts, and London boroughs. For example 39 of the LEAs have the same boundaries as counties, 36 share the same boundaries as metropolitan districts, 32 are the same as the inner and outer boroughs of London, one corresponds to the Scilly Isles, and another corresponds to the City of London. In Wales all eight of the LEAs correspond to the eight counties. These local education authorities derive their power through education committees that are part of the larger government body connected with each LEA. The majority of the members of each education committee are elected officials (councillors), though the professional staff is appointed (Mackinnon et al. 1995).

A variety of models for control of schools can be found in England and Wales. Essentially, there are four: state-maintained, grant-maintained, church-related, and independent. All are accountable to the national Department for Education in varying degrees (Mackinnon et al. 1995).

State-maintained schools (or, simply, "maintained schools") receive their support from the state and are governed by the local education authority. They are the most common school model in England and Wales, though they are decreasing in numbers as a result of the creation of grant-maintained schools by the Education Reform Act of 1988 (Green 1996).

Grant-maintained schools are established when an individual school chooses to withdraw from the local education authority, thereby receiving its support directly from the Department for Education. The decision to withdraw is by the vote of parents and teachers from the school, with election procedures prescribed by the Education Reform Act. The Education Reform Act of 1988, along with the subsequent Education Act of 1993, included some distinct financial incentives for a school community to change its status from "maintained" to "grant-maintained" because of the perception of Parliament that LEAs had become an unnecessary layer of bureaucracy. Moreover, advocates of reform argued that the LEAs were unresponsive to implementing policy changes that Parliament, through the Department for Education, was eager to institute (Green 1996).

Church-related schools are another governance model. The 1944 Education Act resulted in church schools coming under the control of the state, in effect making them "maintained schools." In exchange, the church schools began receiving subsidies to operate the schools from their respective local education authorities. The churches, however, retained control over religious instruction, and their degree of independence from the state varies according to the amount of financial support. Several types of church-related schools have evolved during this century: *controlled schools*, *aided schools*, and *special agreement schools*. Slightly more than 3,000 controlled schools operate through a partnership with their sponsoring churches and local education authorities. The sponsoring church provides the physical facilities and the LEA meets all the other costs. Of course, the school must implement the national curriculum and comply with LEA and Department for Education regulations. Aided schools are a variation on the controlled school, with the sponsoring church providing for a slightly greater share of the operating costs. More than 4,000 schools operate with this status. With aided schools, the LEA appoints a third of the members of the school's board of governors, whereas with controlled schools the LEA appoints a majority. Special arrangement schools, of which there were 77 in 1995, represent yet another type of education partnership between the church and the state, with the state providing for half of the cost of the construction of new church-sponsored school facilities (Mackinnon et al. 1995).

Public education policy is not restrictive. Sponsoring organizations other than churches may organize aided schools or controlled schools. Moreover, any school — secular or religious — may opt for non-maintained status. Many do, and they are known by the general term, *independent schools*.

Independent schools do not receive financial support from the government, relying instead on fees or private endowments for their operation. While independent schools must register with their respective LEAs and are subject to inspection by the Office for Standards in Education, they are relatively free from government regulation. They come in all sizes and varieties, not to mention quality. The most prestigious of the independent schools belong to the Headmaster's Conference, which is composed of some 240 schools enrolling about 159,000 pupils in the United Kingdom (Walford 1986). Another 400,000 children attend 2,249 United Kingdom schools belonging to any of several voluntary associations: Society of Headmasters of Independent Schools (SHIS), Governing Bodies Association (GBA), Girls' Schools Association (GSA), Governing Bodies of Girls' Schools Association (GBSA), and Independent Schools Association Incorporated (ISAI). Only 7% of the school population in England and only 2.5% in Wales attend independent schools (Mackinnon et al. 1995).

Independent schools are diverse, with some among the most expensive in the world and others operating entirely as charities. The whole gamut of education philosophies can be found. Although the Department for Education no longer uses the term "public schools" when referring to independent schools, the expression persists when applied to the schools belonging to the prestigious Headmaster's Conference. Independent schools often are called "private schools," though this term can be confusing because historically a "private school" in England referred to one operated by an individual teacher-entrepreneur (Green 1996).

Finance. The financial system for education in England and Wales is a mixture of local and national government responsibility. Aid to "further education" and "higher education" is disbursed by the national government directly through the Further Education Funding Council and Higher Education Funding Council, respectively. Primary and secondary schools are funded by the local education authorities, though more than half of all expenditures by the LEAs are funded by national grants (Department of the Environment 1994, Figure 107). Overall, the equivalent of 37 billion dollars was spent on education in the United Kingdom in the 1994 fiscal year, with about one-third of that disbursed by the national government and about two-thirds disbursed by local education authorities (Department for Education and Office for Standards in Education 1994, Tables 1-3).

More specifically, primary and secondary schools are funded from three sources. First, the local government, or district council, assesses a council tax. It determines how much of the revenue from this tax will go to the schools in the local community. Second, the national government provides to the district council a revenue support grant. The third is funding from the national nondomestic rate, which is a tax that is collected nationally then disbursed to local districts according to population. About half of a local district's revenue is raised from national sources, namely the revenue support grant program. The remaining half comes from the local district's council tax (Mackinnon et al. 1995).

The local education authority functions as a division of the local government, and a majority of the LEA committee members must be elected district councillors (Mackinnon et al. 1995). Thus the leaders of the local community's school system must compete directly with advocates for other essential community services (for example, health services, public housing, public safety) when the local district allocates its financial resources. In other words, the education budget at the district level in England and Wales is subject to all of the political influences found in state legislatures in the United States.

The Education Reform Act of 1988 greatly diminished the role of the LEAs. First, the Department for Education now must approve the method each LEA uses for distributing its resources among the various schools of the district. The individual schools enjoy much more discretionary authority in the use of their allocations. Each school's governing body decides its own spending priorities and makes its own personnel decisions (Mackinnon et al. 1995). Because a school's budget depends almost entirely on enrollment, the national open-enrollment policy established by the Education Reform Act of 1988 ensures school accountability. Parents dissatisfied with the management of a school simply transfer their children to other schools. Parent choice of schools and school site-based management are prominent features of the

Education Reform Act of 1988. Local education authorities are giving way to the national government on matters of education policy, and they are turning matters of operation over to the individual schools.

Spending on education in England has increased only slightly in recent years. Total funds budgeted for education from fiscal year 1989 to fiscal year 1994 increased by almost 50%. But when calculated as a proportion of total government spending, the amount has not shown appreciable gain for about two decades (DFE and OFSTED 1994, Table 2). During the 1980s education spending actually decreased when calculated as a proportion of gross national product (CIPFA 1993, Figure 6).

The per-pupil cost has increased in the past two decades, with the greatest gains occurring in the amount spent on books and supplies. However, significant variation in the amount spent per pupil occurs from region to region. For example, the 1993 fiscal-year average per-pupil cost for primary education ranged from £1,421 in the rural areas, or "shires," to £2,122 in inner London. The difference for secondary education ranged from £2,100 in the shires to £2,638 in inner London (CIPFA 1993).

In comparison to 16 other industrialized nations, the United Kingdom ranks 13th in per-pupil expenditure. When per-pupil expenditure is calculated in terms of per capita income, the United Kingdom ranks 12th. Only Australia, Ireland, Italy, and the United States rank lower in the proportion of per capita income spent on primary and secondary education (Berliner and Biddle 1997).

Summary

Schools in England and Wales are in a state of transition. Today education occupies a prominent place on the national political agenda, and control of schools is increasingly a national function. Indeed, one must characterize British schools as a national system locally operated.

Beginning in the 19th century and continuing to the dawn of the 21st century, access to formal basic education grew as the nation gained greater consciousness of the needs and hopes of all its citizens, not just its aristocracy. Now, following a wave of education reform that has lasted nearly two decades, schools operate with higher expectations from the government and greater accountability. On balance, the system is improved. Many more students continue to earn secondary-level qualifications, and many more of them continue into further education.

Educators and political leaders are acutely aware of the shortcomings of the nation's schools. All of the fallout of poverty and all of the inequities of a class-conscious society are evident in the schools and classrooms of England and Wales. But the modern history of British education suggests that the nation, especially Parliament and the Department for Education, intends to address its problems. Education policy is front stage in the realm of politics.

CHAPTER TWO

SCHOOLS IN ENGLAND AND WALES: CURRICULA, TEACHERS, AND STUDENTS

Teachers and students define the character of schools. The politics and bureaucracy of education are realities that affect the environment of schools, but the true description of a nation's education system comes from examining what teachers teach, how teachers teach, and whether students learn what teachers intend. This latter point — whether students learn — must be qualified, of course, by issues of equity. In other words, how accessible are education opportunities? In this chapter I pick up the examination of education in England and Wales by looking at the national curriculum, school curricula in general, and the system for assessing student achievement. Disparities in student achievement are considered in the context of social factors. To conclude this two-part examination, I discuss the profession of teaching as it has evolved in England and Wales, because in the end the quality of a nation's education system depends on the quality of the teaching profession.

The National Curriculum

Prior to the Education Reform Act of 1988, the curriculum was entirely in the hands of local education authorities. If the truth be told, it was more in the hands of the head teachers of the individual schools. The only subject required by the Education Act of 1944 was religion, and parents could withdraw their children from those classes if they desired. Although the system of examinations for university admission, which has been in place in some form throughout most of the 20th century, directed much of the secondary education curriculum, only a small proportion of

33

students actually took the exams. Consequently the curricula for both primary and secondary remained discretionary.

The Education Reform Act of 1988 introduced an aggressive course of action by the national government to standardize curricula and student assessment. The national curriculum was instituted for both England and Wales, and eventually it was extended to Northern Ireland. Scotland, which maintains a system of education apart from England and Wales, does not mandate a national curriculum but has a *recommended* national curriculum.

Administration of the national curriculum rests with two national agencies created by the Education Reform Act of 1988. The School Curriculum and Assessment Authority implements the curriculum in England, and the Curriculum and Assessment Authority for Wales is responsible for directing implementation in Wales. The two vary only slightly. Both have the same *core subjects*: English, mathematics, and science. In Wales, Welsh is also a core subject for those schools that use Welsh as the primary medium of instruction. In addition, the curriculum in both England and Wales includes the same set of *foundation subjects*: art, history, geography, music, physical education, and technology. In Wales those schools that use English as the primary medium of instruction require Welsh as a foundation subject. A close examination of the two versions of the national curriculum reveals that the Welsh variation emphasizes a more interdisciplinary approach to content (Pollard 1996).

The national curriculum is prescribed in an intricate system of developmental levels, goals, objectives, themes, and levels of performance. Indeed, the outcry heard from teachers on implementation of the national curriculum had less to do with resistance to the higher standards sought by Parliament than it did with the tedious level of explanation and onerous documentation that the new system imposed. Mackinnon et al. (1995) explained how the curriculum is organized into four *key stages* that cover the years for compulsory schooling:

Key Stage 1 corresponds to the first two years of schooling for children ages five and six.

Key Stage 2 corresponds to the third through sixth years of schooling for children ages seven through 10.

Key Stage 3 corresponds to the seventh through ninth years of schooling for children ages 11 through 13.

Key Stage 4 corresponds to the tenth and eleventh year of schooling for adolescents ages 14 through 16.

Each subject in the national curriculum includes *programmes of study* and *attainment targets*, which are similar to the terms "courses" and "goals" that are in common use in the United States. The national curriculum also makes use of *strands* of ideas that run through each programme of study and through all of the key stages. Figure 1 shows the programmes of study for the core subjects in the English version of the national curriculum (Pollard 1996).

Figure 1. Programmes of study for core subjects.

English	**Mathematics**	**Science**
Speaking and listening	*Using and applying math*	*Scientific investigation*
Reading	*Numbers*	*Life and living processes*
Writing	*Algebra*	*Materials and properties*
Spelling	*Shape and space*	*Physical processes*
Handwriting	*Handling data*	

The strands provide another level of detail for describing the programmes of study by concepts or themes. Some strands are consistent throughout all four of the key stages. Others appear in only some of the stages. In Key Stage 1, for example, the following strands are part of the programme of study on physical processes:

- Electricity and magnetism
- Energy resource and energy transfer
- Forces and their effects
- Light and sound
- The Earth's place in the universe (Mackinnon et al. 1995)

The national curriculum instituted by the Education Reform Act of 1988 caused sweeping change in primary and secondary schools. Where the curriculum had been decentralized and fragmentary, it became at once centralized and uniform. Many British educators continue to believe that the degree of centralization and the precision of description is more harmful than helpful. Indeed, the voice of the teaching profession was strong enough that the Department for Education is encouraging concerted efforts to simplify the implementation mechanisms. The Dearing Report of 1993, which was the official evaluation of the national curriculum by Sir Ron Dearing, chairman of the School Curriculum and Assessment Authority, made a firm case for streamlining the assessment system (Dearing 1993).

Assessment. The complexity of the national curriculum does not end with content. The assessment system is similarly planned in minute detail. For each programme of study there are 10 *levels of attainment* that establish the expected progress each pupil should make from the beginning to the end of compulsory schooling. These attainment levels overlap each key stage. For example, Key Stage 1 includes levels of attainment one through three; Key Stage 2 includes levels of attainment two through five; Key Stage 3 includes levels of attainment three through eight; and Key Stage 4 includes levels of attainment four through 10. *Statements of attainment* describe each of these levels of attainment. However, art, music, and physical education do not use the 10-level system. Instead, they have more general statements of learning outcomes for the end of each key stage (National Curriculum Council 1992).

The level of detail introduced for the national curriculum's assessment system has met with considerable controversy. Frontline educators — teachers and head teachers in the schools — continue to complain that the system is cumbersome and superficial. In response to their outcry, Sir Ron Dearing reported in the first official evaluation of the new system that the scheme relied too heavily on standardized tests. Dearing's report stated that the national assessment system tended to "fragment teaching and learning" and trivialized the process of education assessment to a "meaningless ticking of myriad boxes" (Dearing 1993, p. 61). As a result of Dearing's report, major changes have been proposed for the purpose of simplifying the mechanism for assessment, while keeping the broad goals of standardization and accountability intact.

National Examinations and Qualifications

Assessment is hardly new to the education system of England and Wales. National exit examinations have been a rite of passage for British school children for the past five decades. The General Certificate of Education (GCE), which was instituted in 1951 and later modified in 1965, included three levels of qualifications. The first was the Certificate of Secondary Education (CSE), which was designed so that the top 60% of pupils would pass. The second was the General Certificate of Education (GCE) "O-level" examination, which was designed so that the top 30% would pass. And the third was the General Certificate of Education "A-level" examination system. The O-level examination system was designed to designate mastery of secondary school subjects at age 16; and the A-level scheme was designed to evaluate students at the completion of the sixth form, the year of preparation for admission to higher education. In 1988 the CSE and GCE were replaced by the General Certificate of Secondary Education (GCSE), giving England, Wales, and Northern Ireland a single examination system at the end of compulsory schooling (Mackinnon et al. 1995).

At present, about two-thirds of the pupils in England and Wales pass the General Certificate of Secondary Education. About 30% of the pupils who complete compulsory education subsequently pass one or more A-level examinations. During the past 25 years the proportion of pupils finishing compulsory schooling with either the CSE/GCE or the GCSE has risen significantly, from 34% to 64% (Mackinnon et al. 1995).

In addition to the national system for examinations at the end of compulsory schooling and on completion of the sixth form, numerous qualifications are available in vocational subjects under the aegis of the National Council for Vocational Qualifications (NCVQ). Normally students take an examination for a vocational subject on completing a postsecondary course, which is called "further education" (Mackinnon et al. 1995).

Pupil Achievement

Any discussion of a nation's schools eventually ends in a discussion of pupil achievement. Moreover, the discussion of pupil achievement is always in terms of some type of comparison. The current emphasis in comparative studies of pupil achievement is on two dimensions: international ranking and social inequities. In the case of England and Wales, both kinds of comparisons provide revealing insights.

Cross-cultural comparisons of pupil achievement are fraught with the potential for misinterpretation. As Benjamin Disraeli once said, "There are three kinds of lies: lies, damned lies, and statistics." Actually, the 19th century prime minister's indictment was not so much against statistics as it was a jab at the manipulation of statistics to distort the truth. Statistical comparisons of education systems must respect his admonishment and consider the contextual meaning of any data that are cited. Scope and sequence of the curriculum, the proportion of the school-age population being tested, a nation's investment in education, and socioeconomic variance in the population are just a few of the variables that can affect the comparisons. With this caveat in mind, a general statement can be made that pupil achievement in England and Wales is average in comparison to other nations. Several studies are illustrative.

In a study reported by the Educational Testing Service, the United Kingdom was second in a comparison of five nations (Korea, the United Kingdom, Spain, the United States, and Ireland) for science proficiency among 13-year-olds (Lapointe

1989 as cited in Hlebowitsh and Tellez 1997). In the same report, the United Kingdom was in the middle when the subject tested was mathematics. Assessments of literacy similarly place the United Kingdom in the middle of the nations sampled (Elley 1992).

In strictly national terms, education achievement in the United Kingdom has improved. Between 1979 and 1993 the proportion of pupils who have stayed in school to age 16 increased from 42% to 71%, and the proportion for pupils who stayed through age 18 more than doubled, from 15% to 34% (DFE 1993c). The proportion of pupils who earned qualifications also increased. In 1970 only 34% of the pupils passed O-level examinations, but in 1992 the percentage improved to 64%. Similarly, pupils passing one or more A-level examinations increased during the same time span, from 17% to 30% (Mackinnon et al. 1995). These indicators of achievement, however, contain some troubling inequities when the data are examined closely.

Gender differences. Girls consistently perform better than boys in both the GCSE and the A-level examination. However, the superior achievement by girls is not uniform across the curriculum. Boys outperform girls in mathematics by a slight margin on the GCSE and a large margin on the mathematics A-level examination. The same applies for physics and chemistry, both on the GCSE and the GCE A-level examinations (DFE 1993b).

Despite the fact that women perform better than men in the GCSE and GCE A-level examinations across the board, these differences reverse themselves in higher education. More men than women receive the first degree, and the proportion of men to women increases with advanced degrees (CSO 1994a). This reversal indicates a gender bias against women in terms of English society's expectations for the higher education of women.

Differences among ethnic groups. Analysis of pupil achievement among ethnic groups is difficult because ethnicity was not identified in the national collection of data as recently as 1995. Therefore, observations come from samples taken in conjunction with special reports. The most recent data indicate a high percentage of adults of Pakistani and Bangladeshi origin have not passed the GCSE: more than 50% of the men and 60% of the women. Among Indians, slightly fewer than 40% of the women and slightly fewer than 30% of the men have not passed the GCSE. These proportions compare to fewer than 10% among white adults who have not passed (CSO 1994*b*).

Class distinctions. The class consciousness that is evident in British society shows up in pupil achievement. During the 1950s through 1960s, when the tripartite secondary education system was prevalent, upper- and middle-class children performed better than lower-class children in every measure of education achievement analyzed (Mackinnon et al. 1995). The advent of the comprehensive school system in the 1970s helped to close the gap between the classes, though discrepancies still are observable. Among children from families categorized as "professional," 62% go on to earn university degrees and only 3% do not pass any of the examinations for qualifications — the GCSE or GCE A-levels. However, among the semi-skilled and unskilled working classes, 64% do not pass the GCSE and only 1% goes on to earn a university degree (Mackinnon et al. 1995).

Independent schools. Differences in pupil achievement also appear when independent schools are compared to state-maintained schools. Of course, annual fees at independent schools are high — the equivalent of $19,000 or more. Therefore, the differences in achievement between independent and state-maintained schools also are differences of social class. Even so, they are significant. In comprehensive secondary schools only 12% of the students leave with at least one A-level passing score. By contrast, 61% of the students from independent schools leave with at least one A-level passing score (DFE 1993*b*).

The extent to which the higher performance on A-level examinations by pupils from independent schools is a product of better education or higher socioeconomic status is a question under constant debate. Certainly there is public sentiment that independent schools have their advantages apart from the social-class issue. The original idea for grant-maintained schools — schools freed from the oversight of local education authorities — came from observing independent schools. Also, the government has for a number of years provided an "Assisted Places Scheme," which operates much as vouchers do. Approximately 5% of the independent school enrollment comes through Assisted Places (Mackinnon et al. 1995).

School Life

Any description of a nation's schools, if it is to be complete, eventually must picture school life as seen by pupils and teachers. In the case of England and Wales, very distinctive patterns present themselves, and they make for some interesting comparisons to other nations.

Primary. The best way to understand life in a primary school in England or Wales is to follow a child through a typical day. Imagine yourself as a seven-year-old in this state-maintained English school:

You arrive at 9:00 a.m. and proceed directly to assembly, where all the school children — about 200 — participate in the nationally required, daily act of worship. Everyone is wearing the uniform, a white shirt and the school sweater, and the only differences in dress are the slight variations of shoe style. After the head teacher's concluding prayer at 9:30 a.m., you go to your classroom.

The room is arranged for you and the other students to work in small groups, and you take your seat at your table where four others join you. Because textbooks and workbooks are not commonly used, your teacher directs your attention to the chalkboard, where a set of mathematics problems has been written. The lesson is a continuation of yesterday's, and you begin work, frequently asking questions among the others at your table. When you finish your exercise problems, you and the child next to you begin to work together on a puzzle with brightly colored geometric shapes.

After the mathematics lesson, your teacher reads to your class an excerpt from a German fairytale that also becomes the subject of a writing assignment — rephrasing the moral of the story. Your teacher wants you to use two new words in particular.

At mid-morning, your teacher is replaced by an assistant, who takes you to the playground for about 15 minutes while your teacher goes to the lounge to have tea and conversation with the other teachers. Class resumes promptly at 10:45 a.m. with reading instruction, again organized in small groups.

Your lunch period begins at noon and lasts for an hour. Like most other students, you live within walking distance of your home, so you go there for lunch. Back at 1:00 p.m., your teacher has you begin geography, so your table continues its construction of a wall map of the world for the classroom. The noise level of children coming and going from the supplies shelf doesn't seem to bother the teacher, who is spending most of her time helping another group with the costumes they will use for a skit at the end of the day. You will join the entire class as the chorus when the skit is performed.

At 3:00 in the afternoon, after your teacher dismisses your class, you walk home.

How do educators observing British classrooms characterize them? First they note that they are child-centered, with heavier reliance on integrated, thematic projects than on textbooks or worksheets. Instruction is individually paced. Children have freedom of movement, and there is a more relaxed attitude toward discipline. Another aspect is that pupil evaluation is anecdotal, with the final evaluation written by the teacher in essay form. Teachers do not use letter or number grades to report pupil progress. Also, while the school year is longer than in the United States, actual instructional time is about the same because the day is slightly shorter. In general, the classroom atmosphere is a low-stress environment.

However, primary school life in England and Wales is not without its critics. The national assessment system, which tests pupils at ages seven and 11, was designed to insert more rigorous accountability into the primary school curriculum. Moreover, secondary educators in England and Wales typically complain that students are inadequately prepared for the academic expectations of secondary schools. Undaunted by this criticism, primary school educators defend the student-centered, humanistic approach to education.

Secondary. Secondary schools enroll students from ages 12 to 16, with students having the option to continue their study in the "sixth form" or in a vocational-technical program. The first five "forms" are each one year in length, and the final, or "sixth," form usually is two years long. In contrast to primary schools, the daily routine is more structured and the classroom itself reflects a much more subject-centered focus. The academic year is 190 days, with the vacation schedule similar to the one used by primary schools — six weeks in the summer and shorter vacations interspersed throughout the year. Although a truly typical day is hard to find in a secondary school in England or Wales, given the many varieties of programs, the one that follows describes how the majority of secondary pupils at a state-maintained school in an average local education authority would spend their school day. Imagine, again, that you are the student:

Arriving at 9:00 a.m., your day begins with a short "registration" period, during which there is a schoolwide "daily act of worship." Afterward, you begin a schedule of eight periods of approximately 35 minutes each, with many of the courses using double periods. Thus some of your classes are 35 minutes and some are 70 minutes. Five minutes are allowed to pass between classes, with an hour for lunch. Students are not allowed to drive to school, and so nearly everyone stays on campus for lunch.

Yours is a typically small school (compared to U.S. high schools), less than a thousand students in all five forms; and the extended lunch hour gives you time to relax with your friends and even get an early start on your homework. As in your primary school days, you have a mid-morning break and a mid-afternoon break of about ten minutes. Your teachers look forward to their teatime, and you look forward to the time to let down as well.

Your formal school day ends at 3:30 p.m.; but with about a third of your classmates, you regularly stay after school for activities. The selection is varied, ranging from rugby and cricket to concert band and chamber choir.

As a student in your fourth year of secondary school, you are in the "fourth form." Therefore your curriculum is preparing you for the subject exams you selected for the General Certificate for Secondary Education (GCSE). Your teachers gear the classes to the examinations, and there is a business-like approach to learning because everyone knows that the final grades that really count will be the ones you make on the national tests, not how your teachers grade you on your homework and projects. Those marks are more to help you see where you need to give extra attention.

Like most of your friends, you complain a little about the uniforms and the homework, but they seem to be an established part of the school life. And, just as your parents did a generation before, you still address your male teachers with "sir" and your female teachers as "ma'am." You plan to continue into the sixth form and prepare for the A-level examinations and so reason that at least the homework will pay off in the long run. As a prospective "sixth-former," you will choose three A-level subjects to study in your last two years, when you are 17 and 18. Then, based on your A-level exams, you will go on to a university.

An examination-driven curriculum is not without its problems. Many students who do not plan on attending the sixth form are not motivated for the courses in the GCSE curriculum. Indeed, classroom discipline is a worry among secondary educators, especially in areas that are economically depressed (McAdams 1993). Student disenchantment with secondary education shows up in retention after the compulsory age of 16. Approximately 50% of the students in England and Wales continue full time in some form of further education. This compares to the same proportion of students in the United States who continue in some form of postsecondary education after age 17 or 18. While the comprehensive secondary school has contributed to enlarging access to further education in England and Wales, the British system still trails other nations in retaining full-time students past the compulsory age (McAdams 1993).

The Profession of Teaching

The education reform legislation of the 1980s and 1990s introduced sweeping changes. Parliament restructured local governance of schools, nationalized curriculum and assessment, and targeted the profession of teaching for rejuvenation. As much as any aspect of the British system of education, the profession of teaching is undergoing unprecedented change. Demographically, however, the profile is relatively stable. The majority of teachers are female, with women forming about three-fourths of the teaching force for primary schools and slightly less than half in secondary schools. Minority populations are significantly underrepresented in the teaching profession, according to the Commission for Racial Equality. White teachers constitute more than 98% of the teaching force (Ranger 1988).

Professional roles. Local education authorities in England and Wales employ more than 900,000 persons in the service of education. Of these, more than 500,000 are professional educators (CIPFA 1991). Many professional roles are represented, and each of these roles can be categorized by the level of school control: national, local education authority, or school.

At the national level the most common role is that of *inspector*. Inspection of schools is the responsibility of the Office for Standards in Education (OFSTED), which is a department independent of the Department for Education. Prior to the 1992 Education Act, full-time inspectors from OFSTED conducted all school inspections. Since 1992 OFSTED inspectors play more of an administrative role in conjunction with an inspection system that uses teams of independent inspectors trained in the standards by OFSTED and headed by a *registered inspector* designated by OFSTED (Mackinnon et al. 1995). The new inspection system is not unlike the accreditation system found in most states in the United States.

At the district level a *chief education officer* (CEO) heads each local education authority. Sometimes called a *director of education* for the LEA, he or she functions in much the same manner as a district superintendent in the United States. The position is appointed by the local education committee, which has elected district councillors forming its majority. The chief education officer is assisted by a variety of education officers in varying degrees of subordination: deputy chief education officer, assistant education officer, and administrative assistant. Also, like school districts in the United States, educators holding these positions come from the ranks of teachers. LEAs also employ education specialists, the most common being psychologists and social workers. Given the broad mission for LEAs — one that includes adult and community education — other education specialists are found at the district level. *Career officers*, for example, serve as resource persons for school- or community-based career development programs, and *youth and community officers* provide leadership for neighborhood recreation programs and other community action groups (Mackinnon et al. 1995).

Professional roles in the individual schools also resemble those in the United States. Each school has a *head teacher*, whose duties are like those of a school principal in the United States. Also, most British secondary schools will have a *deputy head teacher*. Because primary school enrollments usually are very small, primary school head teachers rarely will have a deputy and nearly always have some daily instructional responsibilities. The instruction staff consists of teachers, and in secondary schools they might be augmented by laboratory assistants who assist teachers in classes that use laboratory or workshop equipment. *Welfare assistants* will assist teachers with students having special needs who have been mainstreamed into their classes. And larger schools that have the requisite resources will employ audiovisual technicians and media resource officers. *Supply teachers* are employed on a temporary basis when teachers must be absent. Allowing for differences in terminology, the staffing of the education system in England and Wales is similar to the ones found in North America and nations of the European Union (Mackinnon et al. 1995).

Salaries and employment conditions. The Office of Population Censuses and Surveys uses six categories for reporting social class: professional, managerial/technical, skilled non-manual labor, skilled manual labor, semi-skilled labor, and unskilled labor. University professors are considered as professional class, and teachers employed by primary or secondary schools are considered as managerial/technical class (Mackinnon et al. 1995). Salaries for primary and secondary teachers, however, are more on the level of skilled non-manual labor than of the managerial-technical class.

Teacher salaries are governed by the Secretary of State for Education, who consults with local education authorities, teachers unions, and a review board established by the School Teachers Pay and Conditions Act of 1991. In 1994 salaries for teachers ranged from the equivalent of $19,000 to $50,000. Head teachers' and deputy head teachers' salaries ranged from the equivalent of $37,000 to $83,000 (DFE 1994).

Terms of employment and working conditions are stipulated in detail by the 1994 School Teachers Pay and Conditions Document, which is also approved by the Secretary of State for Education. The document very closely resembles a master contract that a local board of education in the United States would agree to with a local teachers association. It spells out everything from the number of hours per year teachers are to be at the school (1,265 hours distributed over 195 days) to the entitlement of a mid-day break without any student supervision responsibilities (Mackinnon et al. 1995). Following are the significant professional duties covered in the School Teachers Pay and Working Conditions Document:

- Prepare lessons.
- Teach classes as assigned by the head teacher.
- Assess student progress and maintain required records of progress.
- Engage in self-appraisal of one's teaching.
- Assist in the appraisal of other teachers.
- Maintain discipline in the classroom and school.
- Communicate with parents regarding their children's progress.
- Participate in inservice required by the LEA.
- Attend meetings called by the head teacher or LEA.

In brief, the professional responsibilities of primary and secondary teachers in England and Wales would be very familiar to most teachers in the United States. A survey of the physical condition of school facilities in England and Wales will find wider variance. While some teachers have the luxury of teaching in modern classrooms with ample textbooks, equipment, and supplies, others teach in dilapidated buildings without enough books for all of their students. Teachers in England and Wales routinely complain that classroom conditions are crowded and capital resources, such as books and equipment, are inadequate for providing high-quality instruction. Because local education authorities control the budgets for education facilities, schools must compete with other public building projects.

Teacher morale is a concern of many educators in England (Green 1996). First of all, salaries have been eroded in terms of purchasing power. During the past 25 years teacher salaries have risen at a rate that is inferior to salaries in other professions. Given that during this same period the British pound was devalued and the cost of living increased substantially, the typical teacher's salary actually decreased. Also, the education reform legislation of the 1980s and 1990s curtailed teacher autonomy on many professional matters, particularly freedom to decide what to teach and how to assess students. The loss of professional prerogative, diminished compensation, and the increased stress from dealing with more frequent and severe classroom discipline problems all have contributed to sagging teacher morale in England and Wales.

Another blow to the professional self-esteem of teachers resulted from the public attitude that seemed to pervade all the reform initiatives. Teachers and the rest of the established education community have been blamed for the perceived ills of the education system. Less attention is paid to the fact that the proportion of students earning GCSE qualifications, A-level qualifications, and university degrees has increased significantly in the past two decades or that the United Kingdom ranks near the bottom in international comparisons of government investment in education. Political arguments on behalf of the education reform agenda targeted the effectiveness and professionalism of teachers specifically, and the message has taken its toll on the morale of the nation's teachers.

Teacher education and professional development. There are two dominant routes for teacher preparation in England and Wales. The first is a four-year university curriculum leading to the Bachelor of Education degree. About three-fourths of the program is similar to a conventional university curriculum, and the remaining quarter is professional education. Another popular track for professional teachers is the Post Graduate Certificate in Education (PGCE). The PGCE is a one-year program, usually based at a university or polytechnic; and it is taken after completing a university degree. The latter is the typical route for teachers who decide on their education careers after leaving higher education. Many polytechnics offer the PGCE program on a part-time schedule for prospective teachers who are working on their teaching credentials while employed full time in other vocations. Either approach must be approved by the Council for the Accreditation of Teacher Education (CATE). At present, slightly more than 60,000 prospective teachers are enrolled in teacher preparation programs, either baccalaureate or postgraduate (Mackinnon et al. 1995).

A recent development in the professional preparation of teachers is the School-Centered Initial Teacher Training program. Begun in 1993, this program allows consortia of primary and secondary schools to receive grants directly from the Department of Education to design and implement their own courses that lead to qualified teacher status (OFSTED 1995). The program was implemented by the Department for Education in response to criticism that teacher training programs based in higher education were too removed from professional practice. Briefly, the program consists of prospective teachers who hold university degrees receiving their initial training directly in the schools. Not surprisingly, schools of education have been critical of the program. It is too early to tell whether school-centered teacher training programs will replace university-based programs entirely. However, the traditional programs already have begun revisions so that curriculum, faculty, and preservice school experiences are more collaborative with local education authorities.

Teacher education in England and Wales has included a support system for first-year teachers for more than a decade. Indeed, many of the induction-year programs implemented by state education systems in the United States were preceded by the British system for assisting teachers in the first year. Teachers and head teachers alike have embraced the induction-year support programs.

A recent development is the growing shortage of teachers. An improving economy in Britain in the past ten years has made it difficult for the teaching profession to recruit or retain qualified teachers, especially in the areas of science, mathematics, and technology. A recent report by the *Sunday Times* (1998) observed that teaching would have to attract at least half of all the mathematics graduates in the nation merely to fill the vacancies for mathematics teachers. Modern languages is another area of acute shortage. With teacher shortages of this scale, the effect of education reform legislation from Parliament is placed in doubt.

Issues and Challenges

At various points in the past two centuries, laissez faire, social reform, local control, and nationalization all have been themes in pubic policy for education. The education reform movement of the past two decades has completed the shift toward a centralized national system of education, and it has amplified calls for accountability. As schools deal with much more intense public scrutiny and the national government assumes a more direct managerial role, numerous issues present themselves. Not least among them will be the national government's claim that it will be more effective than local education authorities in leading the schools into the next century.

Centralizing control. The education reform legislation of the 1980s and 1990s intended to minimize the role of the local education authority. Indeed, critics of the education system have argued that the LEAs had become unresponsive to the nation's call for reform and too remote from the local communities' concerns. Therefore Parliament gave the Department for Education a more direct line of control over policy; and, in turn, individual schools were given more autonomy in their operation. Now, finding and maintaining a proper balance between the national role and the local communities' role will be the challenge. Without question, many educators remain skeptical that the bureaucrats in national agencies will be better than the bureaucrats in the local education authorities. Teachers especially question the wisdom of transferring so many curriculum decisions from the classrooms to national committees. Already there is complaining among teachers that more time must be spent on documentation than on teaching.

Parliament may soon learn that there are two edges to the sword of centralized control of education policy. The ministers of Parliament and the career bureaucrats of the Department for Education are finding it easy to implement their agenda for change now that control is more centralized. Of course, soon they will be expected to begin showing results.

International, multicultural, and bilingual influences. Cultural diversity has two dimensions in England and Wales. First, cultural and linguistic diversity has been a part of the history of the island for centuries. The Irish, Scottish, and Welsh cultures have endured despite a hegemonic Parliament, and only recently has public education policy begun to recognize and encourage their distinctive characters. Now a host of new cultures and languages are part of the education scene. Although England and Wales remain slightly more than 90% white, the proportion of nonwhite students in schools has doubled in the past two decades. Afro-Caribbean, Indian, Pakistani, and Bangladeshi children are the more common minority populations, but political turmoil in the Balkan region has created a steady influx of refugee children with urgent needs. The British education system, especially the schools of inner London and other industrial areas, faces the enigmatic problem of being a British system and educating for

British citizenship but comprising children from the entire international community. Achieving uniformity of purpose in a community of cultural and linguistic diversity has perplexed many nations.

The case of Wales. Ironically, Britain may need to look no further than its own borders for solutions to problems presented by a national curriculum and a multicultural and multilinguistic state. Wales is a case that merits attention.

Anglo-Saxons learned early in the history of England that the Welsh were going to insist on remaining Welsh. After centuries of trying to squelch the language and culture, Parliament's attitude began to change in the latter half of the 20th century. It began to recognize that the United Kingdom is, inescapably, a multicultural society; and the goals of fully integrating regional subcultures politically and socially are not incompatible with the goal of preserving the language and customs of those regional subcultures. In brief, being British and being Welsh are not mutually exclusive; indeed, the cultivation of one should support the health of the other. In Wales, one can be a loyal British citizen and still be distinctively Welsh.

Therefore, Wales has its own governmental agency for the administration of education — the Welsh Office Education Department (Awdurdod Cwricwlwm ac Asesu Cymru). The Office of Her Majesty's Chief Inspector of Schools in Wales is independent of the Chief Inspector in England, and the national curriculum is the responsibility of the Curriculum and Assessment Authority for Wales (Mackinnon et al. 1995).

As a result, Welsh schoolchildren study the same core curriculum as the schoolchildren in England, except in Wales the language of Welsh is a required subject. In addition, the Awdurdod Cwricwlwm ac Asesu Cymru provides specific national curriculum documents for art, music, geography, and history. In those schools where Welsh is the primary language of instruction, then both English and Welsh are core subjects. Where English is the primary medium of instruction, then Welsh is a required foundation subject. The overarching goal for Welsh education is educating children to be bicultural and bilingual — English and Welsh.

Equal opportunity. The thrust of education reform in the past two decades has been centralizing control of the curriculum and increasing the level of accountability. An outcome of heightened attention to assessment, whether intended or not, will be the raised awareness of inequities in the system. Lagging education attainment of nonwhite populations already is well documented; and, as minority populations increase, greater pressure will be applied to the Department for Education to develop programs and policies to close the gap. Moreover, gender inequities in education opportunity after secondary education will continue to receive attention. Analysis of the results from the GCSE and GCE A-level examinations consistently reveals that girls outperform boys, yet women remain underrepresented in university and professional school enrollments. The results of creating a highly focused national curriculum and assessment are predictable: Inequities in educational achievement and opportunity will become more glaring.

The politicizing of public policy on education. Politicians in the British Parliament have learned that education policy is a ripe field for making political hay. But even for a nation whose modern history is characterized by swings back and forth in the politics of public policy, recent years have seen a more intense politicizing of issues in education. If a politician wishes to draw a crowd with strong rhetoric that is relatively immune from backlash, all she or he has to do is criticize the schools and lay blame on the teachers. Similarly, the British press has learned that the education system is an easy mark. As a consequence, newspapers frequently carry sensational exposés of the education system. Headlines such as "A-level Students Can't Distinguish East from West" (*Sunday Times*, 15 August 1999) are common, and they provide ample fodder for members of Parliament. Nowadays both the Labour and Conservative parties use exaggerated claims to promote opposing agendas for reform. Education has become like foreign policy, the economy, or health care — an arena for partisan political debate. Political rhetoric dominates solid research in the debate.

Comparisons to Education in the United States

Similarities. Schools in Britain — whether primary schools or secondary schools — share many of the features of schools in the United States. The bureaucratic organization of schools is very similar, with LEAs comparing to local school districts. In the broadest sense, the curriculum is the same. The primary education consists of core subjects in English, mathematics, and science; and other foundation subjects include history, geography, music, art, physical education, and technology. Parents hold the same aspirations for their children, teachers face the same challenges, and administrators worry about the same problems. Indeed, many of the issues and problems in British education are familiar to teachers in the United States.

Perhaps the most remarkable similarity is the pattern for organizing schools into primary and secondary levels. Moreover, many British LEAs are beginning to adopt the uniquely American pattern of a middle level of schooling for children aged eight to 12. Preschool or early childhood education is optional, though widely supported by parents (nearly half of three- and four-year-olds attend nursery schools or infant classes in the primary schools); and postsecondary education increasingly is seen as a necessity to economic self-sufficiency.

The general level of literacy and education attainment is comparable, with 64% of the pupil population passing the General Certificate of Secondary Education and another 30% passing at least one of the more rigorous A-level examinations (Mackinnon et al. 1995). Approximately 33% of the school population continues into postsecondary education (Mackinnon et al. 1995). In short, formal education is a major current in the mainstream of modern British culture.

Other similarities are evident as well. The British citizenry is becoming increasingly diverse in its cultures and its languages.

Widespread immigration from former British colonies, along with refugees from various Eastern European regions, has resulted in Britain becoming a truly multicultural society. Thus schools have been challenged to meet the needs of a school population that is characteristically different from that of only a generation ago.

A survey of pupil achievement in Britain reveals another, albeit regrettable, similarity. Glaring inequities exist when different social classes and ethnic groups are compared. For example, the percentage of Afro-Caribbeans who pass at least one A-level examination is less than one-half the proportion for Asians or whites. Moreover, children from the middle and higher classes unequivocally achieve higher results than the working class on virtually every criterion (Mackinnon et al. 1995). Indeed, the remnants of Victorian classism are still apparent. In a study of urban British education, Gene Maeroff (1992) observed that class prejudice continues to have detrimental effects on the education and career aspirations of working-class children.

Another noteworthy similarity is the high profile of education in the public forum. The media report education news extensively (usually looking for the sensational), and education reform has occupied much of the public's attention during the last two decades. Between 1980 and 1995 various ministers of Parliament commissioned 14 different "official reports," and three major pieces of education reform legislation have been passed: the Education Reform Acts of 1986 and 1988 and the Education Act of 1993 (Mackinnon et al. 1995). That kind of politicization of education policy rivals even the United States.

Differences. British education differs from the U.S. system in many remarkable ways. Most noticeable is the nationalization of the curriculum and assessment. Also, the example of bilingual education in Wales is very distinctive in comparison to the American approach. And the legal status of religious education has particular differences. In terms of physical facilities, schools characteristically have smaller enrollments and buildings are Spartan, especially in comparison to suburban America.

In England and Wales the patterns for organizing the age levels of schooling are different than in the United States. In particular, compulsory education begins a year earlier and formal preschool education is more prevalent. As a result, the skills and knowledge that educators in the United States normally consider to be represented by a high school diploma are covered on the examination given to British pupils at age 16. Thus the last two years of British "secondary education" are more advanced than the curriculum found in U.S. schools. In fact, a review of the objectives covered on A-level examinations in Britain compares with content found in the College Entrance Examination Board's Advanced Placement syllabi or in a program of general studies at the college level in the United States.

"Literacy first!" could well be the slogan for British primary education. Language development is given priority, and mathematical concepts and skills are taught for mastery. Whole language as a method of instruction seems to be taken for granted, and infant classrooms (equivalent to the primary grades in the United States) are enriched with storytelling and singing and playful activity. At the secondary level the curriculum is very tightly focused on core subject matter, and teachers design their classroom programs exclusively to prepare students for the national examinations, which occur at both age 16 and 18.

Without a doubt, the examination system for secondary education has given the curriculum a very sharp focus; and teachers clearly understand their role in preparing students to succeed. Interestingly, this role has observable effects in the teacher-student relationship in British secondary schools. Secondary teachers are viewed by their students as resources, not as independent arbiters of success. In this regard, the teacher is like a coach; and coach and player have a common opponent — the examination. Of course, teachers cannot really "teach the test," as the test formats are almost exclusively constructed response and essay. Rather, teachers focus on the objectives of the test. Clearly, the system of national examinations is the most evident difference between education in the United States and Britain.

Both the curriculum and the national examination system have affected teacher preparation as well. Elementary teachers usually are prepared in polytechnic colleges. These programs are three years in length, though the degree is equivalent to a four-year baccalaureate in the United States when one takes into account the rigor of the qualifying examinations (the A-levels) for admission. Secondary teachers receive a university education with a major in the subject to be taught, combined with a fifth year of study in a university for the professional certificate, or Post-Graduate Certificate in Education (PGCE). If one plans to teach a subject at the secondary level, one must have mastered the same discipline at the baccalaureate level.

Another important difference between British and American schools is found in the way each approaches bilingual education. The multilingual character of Britain predates the recent arrival of immigrants. Various Celtic dialects were spoken in the British Isles long before English, and Welsh is still the language of commerce in many rural areas of Wales. The response of the British government, at least in the recent history of education policy, is worth noting by other nations with bilingual populations. Recognizing that the Welsh will always insist on being Welsh, as well as English, the Department for Education has empowered the Welsh Office Education Department with all aspects of education in Wales. Among the variations in the Welsh system is the required study of Welsh alongside English throughout primary and secondary education. While the same national curriculum applies to Wales as it does to England, the Welsh have added their own language and literature to the core curriculum. Thus the recognition of the Welsh cultural heritage in the schools of Wales, including the encouragement of the language, is a matter of official policy in the United Kingdom. The people of Wales and the Parliament of the United Kingdom have grown past the ethnic factionalism that plagues some regions of the United States.

Another significant difference in British education when compared to education in the United States is religious education. In the United States religious instruction is banned in public

57

schools; in Britain it is compulsory. The Education Reform Act of 1988 reinforced a similar law passed in 1944, which made religious education a regular part of the curriculum, as well as provided for daily worship services (Mackinnon et al. 1995). Religious education is not included in the national curriculum. Rather, the particular programs of study are left to the local schools to determine.

Summary

Obvious differences exist between British schools and the schools of the United States. The influence of a national curriculum and national system of qualifying exams continues to have an enormous effect on policies and practices at the local level. In brief, the emphasis on accountability results in education reform initiatives focusing more on the product of education than on the process. While uniquely the outgrowth of British history and British culture, these differences provide alternative perspectives to American educators in the continuing discussion of education reform.

CHAPTER THREE

EDUCATION IN SCOTLAND: A TRADITION OF LOCAL CONTROL

The art historian Kenneth Clark observed, "The Scottish character shows an extraordinary combination of realism and reckless sentiment" (Clark 1969, p. 258). He was explaining how a nation so small could have had such a significant impact on science, philosophy, and the arts. His statement also could explain Scotland's ability to forge an education system that works.

Scottish education employs a no-nonsense policy. Goals are sharply focused. Teachers and students are held accountable. And there seems to be a balance in education between the needs of society and the worth and dignity of the individual. A closer examination of the Scottish education system could prove useful to education policy makers in other industrialized, democratic nations. Certainly insight into education in Scotland is needed to understand the larger picture of education in Great Britain.

Scotland is one of the four countries of the United Kingdom. England, Wales, and Northern Ireland are the other three. Provisions for self-government vary among the four, especially because Northern Ireland and Scotland recently established parliaments separate from England and Wales. Reasons for these differences are woven into the individual histories of the United Kingdom's member nations. Compromises and politically expedient solutions have accumulated haphazardly from centuries of territorial conflict. Sometimes, as evident in the violence in Northern Ireland, these political solutions had disastrous consequences in the long run. Other times, the results have served to accommodate constituent nations' identities, as would be the case with Wales and Scotland. Each nation's relationship with the

United Kingdom is the product of its own, unique history. Especially evident in Scotland is a long history — approximately 300 years — of relative autonomy from England in governing its local affairs.

Centuries of war waged by loosely confederated clans against England allowed Scotland to remain independent for most of its early history. During the periods it was not independent, it was, at best, unruly. Even strategic marriages between Scottish and English royal families provided only temporary relief from the seesaw of rebellion and royal reprisal. However, over time both nations sought a permanent peace. In 1707 Scotland became part of the United Kingdom by the Act of Union. When it was enacted three centuries ago, the union called for Scotland to maintain its own legal system and its own national church. In return, the British Parliament became the political entity for ruling the nation.

The 1707 Act of Union also allowed Scotland to provide for its own school system. Having authority over its own schools has proven vital in Scotland's preservation of its national identity and cultural heritage, and it has resulted in the development of a school system that is a model for the rest of the countries in the United Kingdom. When more than a dozen Irish education officials were asked which English-speaking country the Irish consider a leader in education reform, they all answered the same: Scotland (Green 1998). Given the many possibilities — Canada, United States, Australia, New Zealand, England, and Wales among them — their consensus answer is noteworthy.

Scotland was governed by the British Parliament for nearly three centuries, until it formed its own parliament in 1999. However, during the period that Scotland had no legislative body of its own, the country was distinctive in the United Kingdom by its level of autonomy in local government. This spirit of Scottish identity has not waned. Now some Scottish leaders are calling for the status of an independent state within the European Union. Whatever the outcome of that question, Scottish education is certain to remain distinct from the rest of the United Kingdom.

A small country, Scotland's five million people constitute less than 10% of the total population of the United Kingdom. The area is close in size to the state of South Carolina. Like so many states in America that also have clearly distinguishable urban and rural populations, Scotland presents a dichotomy of demographic profiles. On the one hand, it is the most sparsely populated country in the United Kingdom; on the other, there are densely populated urban areas severely affected by poverty. Nationwide, about 20% of school-age children receive public assistance for school lunches. The poverty factor ranges from as little as 6% in the agricultural area known as the "Borders" to as much as 40% in Glasgow. In fact, in Glasgow as much as one-third of the children live in households receiving some form of income support, and approximately one-half receive clothing grants. Unmistakably, the schools of Scotland must serve children who span the entire socioeconomic continuum (Clark 1997a).

Scotland is a homogeneous country. Caucasians constitute 98.7% of the population, nearly all of whom could claim some degree of Scottish ancestry. Of the 1.3% of the population that is non-Caucasian, most are of Pakistani or Indian origin and live in Glasgow or Edinburgh (Clark 1997a). This homogeneity of culture is evident in the organization and control of Scottish schools and in the curriculum and system for assessment.

Organization of Schools

Scottish schools have been separate from those in England and Wales since joining the United Kingdom in 1707. Like education in most of the Western world, the early history of Scottish schools was tied to the church. However, by the mid-19th century, state-supported elementary schools had been established in most of the communities that had enough of a population to support them. In 1885 British Parliament established the Scottish Education Department that, after a succession of name changes, eventually came to be known as the Scottish Office Education and Industry Department (SOEID). The SOEID is supervised by the Secretary of State for Scotland and operates a number of Scottish ministries in addition to its Education and Industry Department work (Clark 1997*a*).

In 1996 local government structures were reorganized into 32 councils. Each of these local councils has an education committee and a director of education. The council education committees are the political sub-division for providing education from nursery school through secondary school. In a very general sense, they are comparable to local boards of education and school district superintendents in the United States. Colleges and universities in Scotland are answerable to the Scottish Higher Education Funding Council (Clark 1997*a*).

Grade-level patterns for schooling. Schools in Scotland follow patterns similar to England and Wales: nursery school, primary school, and secondary school. Compulsory education covers ages five through 16, with primary schools enrolling children for the first seven years (ages five through 12, or years "P1" to "P7"). Secondary schools typically enroll children for the next four years of compulsory schooling (years "S1" to "S4"), though another two years are optional (years "S5" and "S6"). Current education policy in Scotland is stressing early childhood education, known as "Pre-five," and enrollments in nursery schools are increasing (Clark 1997*a*).

In 1996 the Scottish Office Education and Industry Department reported that there were 784 nursery schools, 2,336 primary schools, and 405 secondary schools. A total of 318 schools classified as "special" serve children with special needs, though some of these schools are organized as separate units that share the same facilities as primary or secondary schools. The total school population in Scotland for 1994-95 was 845,440 (SOEID 1996*a*).

Classifications of schools. As in England and Wales, the Scottish primary and secondary schools fall into several categories. Some are state-supported and operated by the local councils; others are state-supported but receive all their funding from the

Scottish Office Education and Industry Department (SOEID), bypassing local council management. And another group is independent of any government control. Each serves a particular niche in the Scottish system (Clark 1997a).

In 1996, when local government in Scotland was reorganized into 32 councils, no provision was made for local school boards. The plan called for the local authority for schools to be included within the local council. The move was controversial, and actual implementation of the new structure for local government has resulted in each of the local councils constituting an education committee, which in effect serves the same purpose as the former board of education. Schools accountable to local councils receive part of their financial support from the central government (through the SOEID) and part from the local council (Clark 1997a).

Grant-aided schools receive their funds directly from the central government (again, through the SOEID). But unlike in England and Wales, where nearly one out of every five pupils at the secondary level attends grant-maintained schools, in Scotland grant-aided schools are few in number. They account for less than 1% of the nation's total school population (Clark 1997a).

Independent schools receive no financial support from the government. However, many of the secondary schools participate in a program of government financial aid for students called "assisted places" — a program that resembles "vouchers" in the United States. Only 4% of school children in Scotland attend independent schools (Clark 1997a).

Cost of schooling. The cost of schooling varies according to several factors. First, education at the secondary level is more expensive than primary education. The average cost per pupil for primary schools is approximately £1,500 (about US$2,200 by the exchange rate at the time this was written), and the average cost per pupil for secondary schools is £2,500 (about US$3,700). However, these amounts apply to schools with larger enrollments. School size also affects the cost per pupil for education. For smaller schools the amounts can run as much as 50% higher (Her Majesty's Inspectorate 1996).

The distinction between large schools and small schools is an important one because so many of Scotland's schools are small. More than half of Scotland's primary schools have fewer than 200 pupils; and in the sparsely populated highlands and coastal islands, there are more than 100 schools with fewer than 20 pupils. A significant portion of the secondary schools — about 15% — enroll fewer than 400 pupils (Her Majesty's Inspectorate 1996).

Curriculum and Assessment Systems

Unlike the other nations in the British Isles, Scotland does not have a national curriculum. Instead, a national advisory body, the Scottish Consultative Council on the Curriculum (SCCC), is responsible for providing continuing, coherent evaluation of the curriculum and assessment systems. The most recent principal document of the SCCC is *Teaching for Effective Learning* (SCCC 1996). The guidelines for curriculum content and method are the product of widespread consultation with teachers, parents, businesses, unions, churches, cultural agencies, political parties, and mass media organizations. These guidelines have become influential in determining the curriculum adopted by schools in local councils. In addition, the Scottish Office Education and Industry Department (SOEID) published its latest curriculum document, *The Structure and Balance of the Curriculum 5-14,* in 1993. Known among Scottish educators as the "5 to 14 Programme," these national guidelines describe the recommended scope and sequence, as well as assessment plans, for the curriculum through primary education and the first two years of secondary education. Reform of the upper secondary years (ages 15 through 18, or years S3 through S6) was proposed recently by the SOEID (1994) in its report *Higher Still: Opportunity for All.* These three documents, each of which resulted from broad community participation, form the foundation for the Scottish curriculum. Moreover, their acceptance at the local level gives testimony to the reputation the Scots have for effectively modernizing their school system (Clark 1997*a*).

Primary curriculum. According to Clark (1997*a*), five broadly described subject areas constitute the curriculum for primary education. They are largely the result of a series of working papers prepared by various groups of professional educators under the auspices of the SOEID. They include:

- English language (including listening, speaking, reading, and writing).
- Mathematics (including problem solving and enquiry, information handling, numbers, money and measurement, shape, position, and movement).
- Environmental studies (including science, social subjects, technology, health, and information technology).
- Expressive arts (including art and design, drama, music, and physical education).
- Religious and moral education (including Christianity, world religions, and "personal search").

The guidelines provide schools with recommendations for emphasis in terms of time allocations and state "attainment outcomes." While most schools follow the guidelines closely, head teachers do have flexibility to plan their own variations to the curriculum. Throughout the curriculum revision process led by the SCCC and the SOEID, the goal was to accomplish a sharper focus and greater accountability in the curriculum without resorting to a nationally prescribed curriculum with mandatory examinations. As a result, several important observations can be made about the Scottish primary curriculum: it is balanced, it encourages interdisciplinary organization, and the assessment system follows the curriculum, rather than vice versa (Clark 1997*b*).

Assessment in primary schools. Primary schools participate in a national system of tests, and individual schools have flexibility in choosing how to use those tests. When the current testing system was implemented in 1991, tests were given to children at the end of the third and seventh years of their primary schooling (ages eight and 12). However, the testing program as it was introduced turned out to be very controversial with teachers and parents, and only about half of the children actually took the tests. Parents and teachers effectively voiced their opposition by their non-participation. As a result, substantive revision in the assessment system occurred. Now much more flexibility is allowed for the time of year the tests are administered and even the year they are administered to children. In effect, the tests are used by teachers as a means of confirming when children have met the "attainment outcomes" at certain levels. As such, their use is more for diagnosis. Unlike in England and Wales, no comparative tables are kept that allow the ranking of schools on the basis of student performance on the tests. Indeed, as the assessment system now operates, such comparisons would not be possible. In primary education, assessment is the responsibility of the teacher and the national testing system is designed to assist the teacher in that capacity (Clark 1997*b*).

Secondary curriculum. Secondary education in Scotland is much more uniform than in England and Wales. The small, homogeneous population of Scotland contributes to consensus on most matters of education policy, including curriculum. Moreover, the fact that only two secondary schools have opted out of local control and less than 5% of the secondary schools are private makes secondary education almost exclusively a state system.

Four national bodies work cooperatively to develop and implement policy that in some way affects the curriculum and how it is taught in Scottish secondary schools: The Scottish Qualification Authority, the Scottish Consultative Council on the Curriculum (SCCC), the General Teaching Council, and Her Majesty's Inspectorate. The Scottish Qualification Authority administers the national examinations for the secondary system; and the SCCC provides guidelines for the curriculum, especially the first four years of secondary school (ages 12 through 16) (Clark 1997*a*). The General Teaching Council is responsible for the preparation and qualification of professional teachers; and Her Majesty's Inspectorate conducts periodic, independent evaluations of schools and reports on various aspects of school quality according to performance standards (Clark 1997*b*). All four bodies work cooperatively; however, the Scottish Qualification Authority is enormously influential given the importance attached to the national examinations. As a consequence of the nature of the examinations, both in terms of content and construction, the secondary curriculum is much more subject-centered than is the primary curriculum.

S1 and S2 years. Even though Scotland does not mandate a curriculum, local councils follow the national guidelines very closely. As a result, the first two years of the secondary curriculum follow a remarkably consistent set of core courses. Courses of study include English, mathematics, physical education, science, social studies (history and geography), creative art, and religious and moral education. Given the similarity to the primary curriculum, critics have argued that the first two years consist merely of review for many students. Critics also add that, for pupils who did not succeed in primary school, the next two grades are years of frustration.

Also, classes are mixed ability. The wide range of student needs that are the result of heterogeneous grouping continues to perplex teachers. Moreover, the remedies have proven more problematic than the original dilemma. For example, concern raised over mathematics achievement, in combination with the policy for mixed ability classes for S1 and S2, resulted in widespread adoption of individualized instruction. Except, in practice, individualized instruction became an over-reliance on commercial workbooks. Many critics of secondary education now describe typical S1 and S2 classrooms as worksheet weary. The strong emphasis on teaching methodology found in the latest wave of Scottish education reform literature, especially *Teaching for Effective Learning*, was a backlash against inappropriate teaching methods used in connection with mixed-ability classes.

S3 and S4 years. Compulsory schooling ends at S4, when students turn 16 years old. However, the majority of students will continue to attend school after the compulsory age. The structure of the third and fourth years of secondary education, S3 and S4, are very similar from school to school. Students begin to make some course selections halfway through the second year (S2); and by the third year (S3), they begin to have even more options. About 90% of instruction time during S3 and S4 is devoted to the core curriculum. Typically, students will enroll in seven to eight courses.

S5 and S6 years. Educators throughout the United Kingdom admire Scotland's upper secondary education (Green 1996). The curriculum is designed with more breadth than elsewhere in Britain, and the schools send more students to universities than elsewhere in the United Kingdom. Of course, one of the reasons that the system seems to work is that Scottish educators agree that improvement is always possible, and dialogue on how to go about improving schools is less politically charged than in England and Wales. Currently Scotland is engaged in a very ambitious reform of upper-secondary education that will implement a more integrated system. Called "Higher Still," the plan for reform will expand opportunities for challenging secondary education to a wider segment of the student population (Raffe 1997).

In brief, courses in the last two, optional years of secondary education will consist of 160-hour courses, with each course comprised of three 40-hour units plus another 40 hours reserved for extended learning (called "induction") or preparation for external examinations. Each unit may be completed separately, and all courses and units are available at five levels: Access, Intermediate 1, Intermediate 2, Higher, and Advanced. To be eligible for enrollment at the advanced level, a student must have completed the prerequisite course with a "credit pass" at the standard grade during the S3 or S4 years. Similarly, students with a "general pass" would enroll at either the Intermediate 1 or the Intermediate 2 level. A key feature of the system is that students may take their courses at a variety of levels. Moreover, the introduction of "Scottish Group Awards" and their companion

"Specialist Group Awards" allow students to integrate study in vocational subjects with the academic courses (Raffe 1997).

Obvious to an outside observer of Scottish education are the several dimensions that are built into the reform program. The first is focus: Core academic subject matter and broadly defined vocational skills are described in recommended syllabi. The second is articulation: The third set of two years (S5 and S6) are intricately connected to the previous two years (S3 and S4, or "standard grade" years). The third is flexibility: Students can study a course at the level that is appropriate. And the fourth is accountability: Success on the external examinations is the motivation for students and teachers to take the system seriously.

Assessment in secondary schools. The Scottish Qualification Authority administers the national examinations for secondary pupils. Briefly, the Scottish Certificate of Education, Standard Grade is given at the end of the statutory four years of secondary education (at age 16) and the Scottish Certificate of Education, Higher Grade is given at the end of either the fifth or sixth year (at age 17 or 18). Students also may sit for the Certificate of Sixth Year Studies, which is the highest qualification offered to secondary students. Many students complete one or more of the increasingly popular Scottish Vocational Education Council modules in lieu of or in combination with the Higher Grade certificate. These modules are competency based and are easily integrated into a student's secondary school course schedule even if the student's intended goal is admission to a university (Raffe 1997).

Curriculum characteristics and development. Two characteristics of the Scottish curriculum distinguish it from others in the United Kingdom. First, it is broader and better balanced than the national curriculum for England and Wales. The Scots have been faithful to the ideal of a liberal education throughout the history of their education system. However, the Howie Report (SOED 1992) found that the last two years of secondary education (S5 and S6) are an exception and that breadth and balance was lacking in comparison to other European nations.

The Scots also adhere to the ideal of comprehensive education in the secondary school. Indeed, when the Howie Report (SOED 1992) recommended a two-track system, the proposal was soundly rejected by the larger education community (Raffe1997). Scottish secondary schools attempt to integrate academic and vocational education, though the English dichotomy between academic and vocational programs remains a powerful force throughout Great Britain. While Scottish educators speak with pride about the comprehensiveness of the secondary education system, there are de facto remnants of academic and vocational tracks.

Several factors are noteworthy when discussing the continuing development and evaluation of the Scottish curriculum. First, Scots take a strong interest in education policy, both at the local and the national levels. Moreover, in the main they are confident that the education system is effectively serving the Scottish nation. These points are important because they allow the continuing public debate on education policy to occur without the demagoguery or acrimony that so often is present in other nations. In addition, the major stakeholders in Scottish education — parents, teachers, churches, businesses, and unions — all assume responsibility in the participatory process of curriculum development. Crucial in this process has been the role of the education community, especially primary and secondary teachers. They expect to, and do, assume the role of leadership. Most important, the centralized authorities (the SOEID, the SCCC, the General Teaching Council, and the Scottish Qualifications Authority) play vital roles in the change process. On the whole the system works. There is diverse opinion and spirited debate, but cooperation and the goal of consensus are prominent characteristics (Harrison 1997).

Special education. For the past 25 years Scotland has provided a free public education to all children regardless of their special needs. Approximately 24,000 students (about 3% of the student population) receive some kind of instruction in connection with their special needs. Since the Warnock Report (Department for Education and Science 1978), special education has been provided mostly in mainstream settings. However, there are special schools operated by local councils or as grant-aided schools. In all, there are 201 special schools in Scotland enrolling about 9,000 students. An additional 1,200 students receive instruction in special units attached to primary or secondary schools. Another 14,000 students receive special instruction while attending mainstream classes (Closs 1997).

In schools operated by local councils, special education takes one of three forms: special resource units (or separate classes), learning support teachers who assist special students attending regular classes, and special support services (for example, medical and psychological services required in connection with the special learning needs). While there is no requirement in Scotland for special education teachers to have special credentials, about one half do. Special teacher credentials are available for school psychologists, auxiliary staff (for example, nurses), and teachers. All, of course, must have regular primary or secondary teaching credentials (Closs 1997).

Great strides have been made in Scottish special education in the past 25 years, though Scottish educators are quick to point out that concerns still remain. In particular, children with social or emotional disabilities are not integrated into the same assessment and identification system as are children with cognitive or physical disabilities. Rising rates of exclusion for children who probably have special needs reveal a gap in special education policy. In addition, little thought has been given to the unique problems of assessment, identification, and service for bilingual children who have special needs. Bilingual children are small in number and they are scattered widely about the nation, making the problem even more difficult. Finally, children who are excluded for health reasons do not have the legal right to education services outside school as do children in England and Wales. In Scotland there exists a public policy loophole that denies free and appropriate education for some children (Closs 1997).

Curriculum and the Scottish Identity

Cameron Harrison explained that we can use three contexts for examining "how Scottish is the Scottish curriculum" (1997, p. 156). First, we must look at the content. Next, we consider the characteristics, or "nature," of the curriculum. And third, we should observe the process of curriculum development. The importance of the "Scottishness" of the curriculum and its relationship to the broader education goals of the United Kingdom is best captured by T.S. Eliot's observation on the differing cultures of Great Britain.

> it is to the advantage of England that the Welsh should continue to be Welsh, that the Scots Scots, and the Irish Irish. . . . If other cultures of the British Isles were wholly superceded by English culture, English culture would disappear too. (Eliot, "Notes toward the Definition of Culture," cited in Harrison 1997, p. 156)

The Scots have done their part to enrich British culture by first enriching their Scottish heritage, and the school curriculum has played a vital role.

Scottish content. Scottish language and literature, in combination with Scottish history, distinguishes the curriculum from others in the United Kingdom. While Scotland does not require separate courses in Gaelic, students study about their ancient language in courses on Scottish culture. In addition to Gaelic, when students read the literature of Scotland, they are introduced to "Scots," which is a dialect of English that is sufficiently distinct that it nearly qualifies as a separate language. Educators might ask why a nation would find it important to sustain traditional languages that are nearly extinct. Paradoxically, the answer lies in the increasingly widespread acceptance of English as the medium of international commerce. According to Harrison (1997), the more the people of a nation become internationalized, the more important local identity becomes. Citing the smaller nations of the European Union as examples, all of which are becoming increasingly bilingual, Harrison observed that a modern education system now has a two-fold purpose in language education. It must ensure that the nation can be vital in global commerce, and it must simultaneously ensure that its national heritage preserves its unique linguistic and literary richness. In this respect, Scotland is no different from Ireland or the Scandinavian countries.

Gaelic schools. Unlike Wales or the Republic of Ireland, Scotland was late in coming to the rescue of its traditional languages. Today less than 2% of the people of Scotland are literate in Gaelic, with most of them concentrated in the remote Western Isles, the Highlands, or the Strathclyde regions (Clark 1997*b*). The primary schools of Scotland, however, have been the main instrument in reviving the language. During the 1996-97 school year, approximately 1,500 students were enrolled in Gaelic schools — a figure that has shown marked increase since the Scottish Office Education and Industry Department began policies to encourage their development (Clark 1997*a*). While most of the Gaelic schools are scattered throughout rural areas, some also are located in the larger cities: Glasgow, Edinburgh, and Aberdeen.

The principal objective of Gaelic schools is for students to gain equivalent fluency in Gaelic and English by the end of their primary school education (normally, age 11). The medium for instruction in all subjects is Gaelic through the first three years of primary education. Then English is introduced gradually. This emphasis on bilingual fluency is not at the expense of the other subjects, however. Gaelic-medium schools follow the same curriculum guidelines as do other schools. In this connection, the Scottish Office Education and Industry Department has funded a number of research studies to compare student achievement levels between English-medium and Gaelic-medium schools, though the reports are only beginning to be released (Clark 1997*b*).

The Profession of Teaching

Important strides have been taken in the past 40 years toward improving the professional status of teaching. The status of teaching was at low ebb in 1961, when teachers in Glasgow staged a strike over poor working conditions and declining education standards. Now, at the turn of the 21st century, they hold a renewed sense of professionalism. According to Clark (1997*c*), a significant element in the emergence of teaching as a profession in Scotland was the establishment over 30 years ago of the General Teaching Council.

General Teaching Council. The General Teaching Council is the national policy and regulatory body for preparing and licensing ("registering") teachers for nursery, primary, and secondary schools. It represents all the public interests in education, not just those of teachers. Teachers are the largest constituent group on the council; 30 members are elected from the ranks of registered teachers (Clark 1997*c*).

The General Teaching Council is responsible for maintaining a list, or registry, of teachers eligible to teach in public schools in Scotland. Given that it is illegal for any school in the public sector (approximately 95% of all schools) to employ a teacher who is not registered with the General Teaching Council, its role is central in the Scottish education system. Moreover, all lecturers in colleges of teacher education must also maintain active registration with the General Teaching Council (Clark 1997*c*).

The General Teaching Council plays a prominent role in ensuring high quality in the Scottish education system. Its responsibilities resemble those of a state professional standards board in the United States. Although not inclusive, the following list indicates the widespread influence and significance of the council's role in education. The council:

- Maintains the registry of teachers eligible for employment in public schools.
- Conducts a continuing analysis of data for the supply and demand of teachers in primary and secondary schools.
- Regulates the admission of teachers trained outside Scotland to the registry.

- Conducts disciplinary hearings for registered teachers accused of misconduct.
- Oversees teacher preparation programs in higher education (Clark 1997c).

Teacher education. The backlash against teacher education that has accompanied education reform in other nations is absent in Scotland. As reflected in Scotland's rather explicit policy on teacher qualifications, preservice teacher education is valued. The Scottish Office Education and Industry Department (1996b) reported that 10 institutions offer some kind of curriculum for initial teacher preparation, and the programs are perceived to be high in quality (Clark 1997c).

Three separate paths to teacher qualifications are possible in Scotland. A four-year course of study leading to the bachelor of education degree is most common for primary teachers. It consists of a program of liberal education along with professional studies and practical experience in schools. Secondary teachers generally choose a combined degree program consisting of a bachelor's degree in a subject area and a course of study in professional education, including practical experiences in schools. Either primary or secondary teachers may choose to pursue the one-year "Post Graduate Certificate in Education" (PGCE), which follows a four-year bachelor's degree. The PGCE is popular for persons who decide after their university studies to complete a course of study leading to teacher qualifications. In addition, four-year bachelor of education degrees are available in music, physical education, and technology education (Clark 1997c).

As a rule, requirements for entrance into teacher education programs are high. Jokes about "those who can do, those who can't teach" are not heard in Scotland, because the standards for entry into the profession typically are higher than others requiring a bachelor's degree. For example, beginning in 2000 the General Teaching Council's minimum requirements for admission to a B.Ed. program require "higher grade" passing scores on the Scottish Certificate of Education examinations in four subjects, one of which must be English and one of which must be mathematics (Clark 1997*c*). In terms meaningful to educators in the United States, this is roughly equivalent to passing four of the College Entrance Examination Board Advanced Placement Examinations with high enough scores to receive advanced placement credit. Minimum requirements for the Post Graduate Certificate of Education, in addition to requiring a university degree, are similarly rigorous.

Professional development. For the past decade, teacher education policy has given greater importance to inservice professional development. In 1984 the National Committee for the In-service Training of Teachers created a program with three tiers. The first tier includes certificate courses, usually one term in length. A second tier includes inservice delivery of bachelor's of education courses offered by colleges of education for teachers who wish to add qualifications. And a third tier is the master's of education degree offered by universities, consisting of the equivalent of four terms of full-time study. The National Committee for the In-service Training of Teachers, in creating its strategy for encouraging formal programs for professional growth, followed national guidelines for the courses. In addition, it built in a system of external evaluation and quality assurance for the programs. Thus professional development in Scotland is a coherent program — one that involves the active cooperation of local schools, colleges of education, and universities (Clark 1997*c*).

Comparisons to Education in the United States

Education in Scotland has many similarities to education in the United States. In fact, schools in Scotland have more in common with those in the United States than they do with schools in England and Wales. The most evident shared characteristic is local control. Increasingly, education is becoming a national function in Great Britain. Scotland is the exception. As a result of the Act of

Union in 1707, Scotland has enjoyed the same broad powers over its school system as do states in the United States. Moreover, the local political subdivisions of Scotland have education committees that operate similarly to local boards of education in the United States.

Other similarities occur as well. The national curriculum in Scotland, technically, is advisory. The use of the national assessment system is optional. As a consequence, schools are not ranked on the basis of student performance on the examinations. Indeed, Scots have resisted vigorously any movement toward the kind of mandatory curriculum and testing found in England and Wales, especially in their primary schools.

The professional preparation of teachers in Scotland resembles the design of teacher education in the United States. In both countries there are options for completing a teacher education program at both the baccalaureate and post-baccalaureate levels. National guidelines for course content, teacher competencies, and assessment for entering teachers play a prominent role. And school and higher education partnerships for providing classroom experience for teacher candidates are central to teacher education programs, just as in the United States.

The General Teaching Council is another aspect of Scottish education that is similar to education in the United States, at least in those states that have a professional standards board for teaching. The teaching profession has a strong voice in all matters affecting the quality of teaching in Scottish schools. Through the General Teaching Council, the profession has been instrumental in implementing many of the reforms of the past two decades.

Differences in the two systems abound, of course. First, in the public debate on education reform, Scotland has succeeded in avoiding the level of rancor that has been seen in England and the United States. Policy grows out of consensus-building among broadly representative national councils, rather than the shrill rhetoric of political campaigns.

Especially notable among the differences in Scottish schools and those in the United States is size. The average enrollment for secondary schools is 800 pupils, and only 550 for primary schools. The small size of schools, however, does not mean insufficient professional resources. A typical secondary school of 800, for example, will be staffed by a head teacher, one deputy head teacher, three assistant head teachers, about 16 "principal teachers" (department heads) for subject areas, three or four "principal teachers" for guidance, and a complement of classroom teachers sufficient to keep class sizes below the statutory maximum. What these smaller Scottish schools do not have are amenities. School facilities do not include the auditoriums, stadiums, arenas, natatoriums, studios, laboratories, or telecommunications systems, all of which can be found in most American schools. Scottish school physical plants are unimposing, and equipment is sparse. Clearly, the focus is on a core academic curriculum.

A focused curriculum, no doubt, explains how the Scots can manage to spend less per pupil than do schools in the United States. They do not try to do too many things; but what they decide to do, they do well.

Notable differences in the curriculum also can be found. In the primary schools the emphasis is on literacy — verbal and mathematical. Other subjects are introduced, of course, but the curricular target is undisputedly what Americans refer to as the three R's. The Scots add a fourth "R" to the list, religion.

Religious study is included in the national guidelines for curriculum along with social studies, environmental studies, the arts, and physical education. Also, the Scots do not labor over methodological debates to the same extent as do teachers (and, regrettably, lawmakers) in the United States. Ask a Scottish primary teacher whether reading should be taught by way of "phonics" or "whole language" and the response likely would be a surprised, "Both, of course! Why would you ask?" As in England and Wales, the classroom environment of the primary school is student-centered with an activity-oriented curriculum.

At first glance, secondary education in Scotland seems very American, especially considering the Scots' dedication to the concept of comprehensive schooling. However, several very noticeable differences appear on further examination. First, there is no middle school organization, as Americans would understand it. After primary education ends at age 12, students advance to the secondary school, where they attend four more years of compulsory education (ages 12 through 16). The final two years of secondary education (ages 16 to 18) are optional. Second, extracurricular activities, especially sports, do not encroach upon the main mission of secondary schools. Expense is minimal, with programs emphasizing "club" level participation.

The most significant difference between Scottish secondary schools and those in the United States is seen in the role external examination plays. The Scottish Qualification Authority administers the exams leading to the Scottish Certificate of Education at Standard Grade and the Scottish Certificate of Education at Higher Grade, therefore course content and standards are closely regulated. Given the prominence these examinations play in admission to higher education or desirable employment, classroom instruction is characterized as very businesslike. Students understand what they need to do, and their teachers play the role of facilitating their success.

The teacher's role is significantly different in many ways, actually. The development of education policy, especially in the past two decades of reform, includes the teaching profession in meaningful fashion. While teachers or teacher unions do not drive public education policy, both are viewed as indispensable stakeholders. And on policy issues affecting curriculum, instruction, and assessment, the public looks to the professional community of teachers for leadership. Related to the value the public gives to teacher opinion on professional matters is the acknowledgment that teachers have both expertise and experience that the rest of the population does not. In Scotland, the notion that anyone who knows enough about a subject can teach it is an anathema to a principle that seems to guide Scottish education: The system is only as good as its teachers, classroom to classroom.

The importance the Scots give to professionalism in the teaching force is in stark contrast to those states in America that routinely control teacher shortages by issuing "emergency" or "alternative" credentials. In Scotland, schools cannot employ a teacher who has not completed a teacher education program approved by the General Teaching Council. Moreover, graduates of Scottish colleges of education and school administrators alike affirm the value of teacher preparation. Unlike the United States and even England and Wales, where teacher education programs often are accused of being the source of public education's ills, Scottish colleges of education are respected partners in the education system.

Summary

The work of social institutions is, by their nature, organic; and how a nation educates its youth reflects an institutional "state of mind." In Scotland the institution of formal education reflects its unique history in relation to the rest of the United Kingdom and its own national culture. It is both British and Scottish, which the Scots do not see as a contradiction in terms. Staunchly grounded in principles of liberty and showing a predilection toward organization and efficiency, Scottish educators deserve the reputation they have earned for operating an education system that works. The largely homogeneous population agrees on central purposes and aims of education, and public policy is more the product of cautious consensus-building by national councils and advisory groups than of partisan politics. Schools are locally controlled, and the "national curriculum" is actually advisory to the local councils, though at the secondary level, external examinations for the certificates result in a fairly uniform approach to content and standards for achievement.

Scottish educators agree that their schools face many challenges. The educational fallout of poverty so apparent in the larger cities — low achievement, disruptive behavior, and higher incidence of special needs — plagues schools in Scotland just as it does in the United States. Poverty's downward spiral results in minimal public funding of education, and inadequate fiscal resources limit how local councils are able to address the issues. Still, Scotland makes for an informative case study of how a nation can effectively balance its national interest in education with its tradition of local autonomy.

CHAPTER FOUR

NORTHERN IRELAND: STRIVING TO OVERCOME HISTORY

The province of Northern Ireland began as a bitter compromise. When the Republic of Ireland was established in 1921 after its war for independence, England resented the notion of an independent Ireland. Concurrently, the Irish loathed the fact that peace negotiators granted part of their island to England. The only reason the Irish accepted this compromise was because they believed it would be temporary.

Temporary solutions have a way of becoming the status quo, which has been the case with Northern Ireland. Moreover, the underlying social problems that prevented a permanent solution are rooted in history. Under the governance of the British Parliament and the English Protestant majority solidly in control of commerce, little progress occurred in the six counties that form Northern Ireland through the remainder of the 20th century. Catholic Irish society in Northern Ireland retreated into parochial communities under the institutional prejudice supported by British law. Dissent festered and riots and reprisals occurred with regularity. Civil unrest raged during most of the last half of the century. Today, in spite of efforts such as the Good Friday Peace Accords of 1998 and the establishment of a parliament for Northern Ireland, the nation still teeters between war and peace. Indeed, even the status of the parliament remains off-again, on-again as the troubled state tries to heal itself. The hope is that a greater degree of political autonomy for Northern Ireland will invite more equal participation by the Catholic Irish in the legislative and policymaking process. The fear is that old prejudices deeply rooted in the consciences of people do not die with the adoption of new articles of government.

The place of schools in this brief history of Northern Ireland, while not very conspicuous, is certainly significant. The education system since the beginning of the nation's history has been segregated, Protestants attending the state schools and Catholics attending parochial schools. This bifurcation invites a closer look. The question we must ask is whether the schools merely reflect society's prejudices or whether they contribute to it.

A History of Segregated Schools

The national schools of Northern Ireland have their beginning in the national Irish school system, established in 1831 by Lord Stanley, then the Chief Secretary of Ireland (Akenson 1970). In his brief history of church-state relations in the schools of Northern Ireland, Seamus Dunn (1993) noted that the system had evolved into three separate parts by 1920, when British Parliament adopted the Government of Northern Ireland Act. In a tripartite system, the national schools were comparable to the primary schools of England, and the intermediate schools were parallel to secondary schools. In practice, the parts operated independently of one another. Moreover, the national schools, though funded in part by the state, actually were operated by local churches. Thus the system was as much parochial as public, and the schools were either Protestant or Catholic. The third part of the system was composed of technical schools, which were few in number and never much of an influence in the nation's early history.

Given the 400-year history of relations between Protestant Britain and Catholic Ireland, the history of education in Northern Ireland is a history of two separate school systems in which both religious communities have protected their interests with the kind of intensity that leads to intolerance. The system that emerged was the product of vitriolic dialogue and enduring distrust on both sides.

Dunn (1993) also made the case that historically, whenever British law and public policy saw fit to treat the two systems differently, it was the Catholic schools that suffered discrimination. The national schools, which became de facto Protestant schools under the government of Northern Ireland, enjoyed the advantage. A closer examination into how this division began is necessary to understand the state of the education system today.

The foundation of today's bilateral school system can be traced to Northern Ireland's first official report on education — the Lynn Report. Filed in 1922, the Lynn Report was the product of a committee appointed by the first minister for Northern Ireland, Lord Charles Londonderry. Its central purpose was to recommend the structure for a national school system of the new nation. Significantly, the committee included representatives of the Protestant churches and the Unionist Party. Also significantly, representatives of the Catholic Church were invited to participate, but declined. While historians might argue whether it was bad judgment on the part of the Catholic bishops to opt out of the Lynn Committee deliberations, most agree that they did so because of their suspicion that the Unionists would draft most of the recommendations. The Catholic bishops did not want to give the appearance that they agreed to a document that might and ultimately would be used against Catholic schools (Dunn 1993).

Essentially, the Lynn Report recommended three kinds of schools for primary children. First would be local authority schools, also known as state schools. Second would be those called partially controlled state schools, which later came to be known as four-and-two schools (four of the controlling board members were from the local authority and two were from churches). Third, another type of school was to be the voluntary schools, which were schools independent of state control (Dunn 1993).

Another aspect of the Lynn Report that proved crucial was its recommendation on funding. The amount of state funding for education was to be in proportion to the degree of local control. Thus the state schools received full funding and the voluntary schools received none (Dunn 1993).

While the funding formula by itself seemed innocuous enough, its effect was devastating to the Catholic community. Because many of the Protestant schools had transferred their control to the state, they were to receive full funding under the Lynn recommendations. And because the Catholic schools would likely remain independent, they were to receive none. Moreover, historians have described passages in the Lynn Report that addressed religious education as assuming that the state schools would be Protestant schools. This, of course, left Catholics little choice about which schools to patronize. Even though the report stated that religious education in state schools would be open to children of all religious denominations, the first schools of the nation of Northern Ireland were assumed to be divided along religious lines, with one religion to be given preferential financial treatment (Dunn 1993).

When the Lynn Report made its way into legislation in the form of the Education Act of 1923, the part dealing with religious education in the state schools was tempered so that whatever religious education took place was not compulsory and not provided by the local education authority. A voluntary school, on the other hand, was free to provide religious education along any lines of doctrine that it chose. State schools, then, were not legally defined as Protestant, nor were voluntary schools legally defined as Catholic. Indeed, Lord Londonderry was committed to a state school system that was nondenominational. His authority was nothing less than the Government of Northern Ireland Act of 1920 that prevented the establishment of a national religion. But, given the Protestant history of the schools that changed to local authority control (state schools), everyone assumed that Protestants would be attending them. The voluntary schools, then, became the Catholic schools (Dunn 1993).

Legislation in the years following the Education Act of 1923 did little to relieve the tension between the two religious communities, which continued to entrench in two separate school systems. Unionists successfully pressed for a stronger Protestant presence in the state schools, making it possible for Catholics to argue for state funding of voluntary schools. Through the debates, Unionists stood firm for a state school system open to all children, albeit one with Protestant teachers and Protestant religious education. The Catholics also were resolved, standing for a separate school system for Catholics that would be Catholic in all respects (Dunn 1993).

Finally, the Education Act of 1930 was passed to settle the issue. Like the treaty that brought the country itself into existence, the Education Act of 1930 was an uneasy compromise that merely institutionalized distrust. Unionists were satisfied that state schools finally reflected the Protestant and British ethos in all respects. And Catholics received half-funding for their voluntary schools. The division was official (Dunn 1993).

The Education Act of 1930 also made it official that the de facto Protestant schools would be funded at twice the level of the de facto Catholic schools. While the gap in funding has diminished over the decades, it remained in place as late as the 1990s (Cormack et al. 1991).

Today the two systems are close to being evenly divided in terms of enrollment, and there is some evidence that the system will become integrated soon. The future of public education policy is open to conjecture, but any new initiatives will have a long history of institutionalized segregation they must strive to overcome.

School Organization and Control

The central government agency responsible for education in Northern Ireland is the Department for Education Northern Ireland (DENI). The minister of education, a member of the Northern Ireland Parliament, is the chief spokesperson for education policy.

Curriculum and assessment is the responsibility of the Council for the Curriculum, Examinations, and Assessment (CCEA). Its chief purpose is to advise schools on the content of the curriculum. CCEA also administers the national assessment system to monitor pupil progress through the primary years and administers examinations to students at various levels on completion of secondary school or grammar school.

The organization of schools is complex, reflecting decades of conflict between the Irish Catholic and Unionist Protestant communities, but several distinct categories can be defined.

Controlled schools. Controlled schools are fully funded by the state and under the control of Education and Library Boards (ELB). The education and library boards, which are managed by boards of governors, are similar in function to local boards of education in the United States. A controlled school's operating expenses (salaries and supplies) and capital expenses (buildings and equipment) are met by the local ELB. As a result of the history of controlled schools, with few exceptions, students and faculty are Protestant. Controlled school status may be for primary schools, secondary schools, or grammar schools. They do not charge tuition or fees for attendance (Osborne 1993).

Voluntary maintained schools. These schools are independent of the control of the education and library boards, and their boards of governors include a majority of representation from the sponsoring organization — usually the Catholic Church. The local ELB provides the operating expenses and the DENI (Department for Education Northern Ireland) may approve grants for capital expenditures for up to 85% of the cost. Voluntary maintained schools could be either primary or secondary. They do not charge tuition or fees for attendance (Osborne 1993).

Voluntary grammar schools. Northern Ireland operates a dual system of secondary education, with secondary schools and grammar schools forming the two parts. Voluntary grammar schools are highly selective secondary schools, with only about 40% of eligible-age pupils gaining acceptance. Thus the system has two tracks, with the upper track having an elitist character. Usually churches or other religious organizations sponsor and manage voluntary grammar schools through a board of governors (Osborne 1993).

The Department for Education Northern Ireland (DENI) funds all the operating costs of voluntary grammar schools, and it funds

85% of the capital expenditures. Boards of governors of voluntary grammar schools may assess miscellaneous fees for pupils who attend (Osborne 1993).

Integrated schools. The Education Reform Order of 1989 introduced initiatives to encourage integration of the Protestant and Catholic communities. Two new classifications of schools were created for the explicit purpose of promoting integration. Controlled integrated schools come under the governance of ELBs, and grant-maintained integrated schools are under the direct supervision of the Department for Education Northern Ireland. In both instances, boards of governors must ensure that the faculties and student bodies are equally represented and the schools' programs support the goal of an integrated society (Dunn 1993).

The support for integrated schools is growing. A series of surveys conducted over the past two decades shows that a majority of the population of Northern Ireland is in favor of the concept of integrated education. However, only a small proportion of parents who say they favor the concept indicate that they would actually transfer their children into an integrated school (Cairns et al. 1993).

The Council for Catholic Maintained Schools. A very recent development in the organization of the national system of schools is the Council for Catholic Maintained Schools (CCMS). Established in connection with a broad field of reforms in 1989, the CCMS is responsible for coordinating plans and programs for the voluntary maintained schools under the aegis of the Catholic Church. The Department for Education Northern Ireland funds operating costs of the CCMS and provides for substantial support for capital costs (Osborne 1993).

Reform: Reflections of the Past and Hope for the Future

Public policy for education in Northern Ireland has been an extension of England's since the 19th century. It is not surprising, then, that Northern Ireland's Education Reform Order of 1989 mirrored the reform legislation for England and Wales that had been adopted the previous year. Several themes found in the Education Reform Act of 1988 for England are evident in Northern Ireland's Education Reform Order of 1989. The first is a stronger national hold on the curriculum. The second is parent choice of schools. The third is the local option of transferring control of a school from local districts into direct supervision by the school's own board, which then is accountable to the national education agency (in Northern Ireland, the Department for Education Northern Ireland; in England and Wales, the Department for Education). In both cases reform was intended to address a perceived decline in standards. And, in both cases, the driving force behind many of the changes was a belief that market values would stimulate higher levels of performance.

However, another dimension was added to education reform in Northern Ireland — Catholic and Protestant relations. The Education Reform Order of 1989 represents an increasing awareness that segregated schools promote the social division that has left the country ravaged, and it contained two provisions that opened wider the channels for dialogue. First, the Council for Catholic Maintained Schools was established to facilitate coordination of the Catholic sector of voluntary maintained schools and to invite more direct participation by Catholic leaders in the policy decisions of the Department for Education Northern Ireland. While policy analysts might argue that the creation of the CCMS only serves to underscore the division between Protestant and Catholic schools, the immediate effect has been a strengthening of the Catholic voice in policy decisions that affect children in Catholic schools. That action alone gives some promise for improving relations.

The Education Reform Order of 1989 also introduced mechanisms for promoting schools with integrated faculties and student bodies. The effort is long overdue, as only 1% of all schools in Northern Ireland can be said to be truly integrated (Osborne 1993). The reluctance of the people to integrate notwithstanding, the fact that the official policy of the government of Northern

Ireland now promotes integration and tolerance must be viewed only as progress.

As the new century begins, Northern Ireland is reforming its education system in a way that both reflects the past and offers hope for the future.

Curriculum

The Education Reform Order of 1989 followed closely the reform legislation in England and Wales from the previous year. Indeed, the same terminology is used: "key stages," "programs of study," "level descriptions," and "attainment targets." The curriculum is definitively national in its character, as all schools are expected to follow it and the assessment of all pupils aged four through 16 is based on it. The primary goals of the curriculum are expressed in the text of the Education Reform Order:

- Promote the spiritual, moral, cultural, intellectual, and physical development of pupils at the school and thereby of society; and,
- Prepare such pupils for the opportunities and experiences of adult life (CCEA 1999*a*).

Key stages. Four key stages define the curriculum. Key Stage One is devised for children ages four through eight (school years one through four). Key Stage Two includes children eight through 10 (school years five through seven). Key Stage Three includes children aged 11 through 14 (school years eight and nine). Finally, Key Stage Four is organized for children aged 14 through 16 (school years 11 and 12) (CCEA 1999*a*).

The curriculum is organized to facilitate a national system for assessing pupil progress. Subject matter is organized to ensure that essential skills and concepts are covered, and the objectives are prescribed with a very high degree of specificity. Programs of study, attainment targets, and level descriptions provide the framework for understanding the mandatory curriculum.

Programs of study. "Programs of study" refer to the content of the curriculum. While schools are free to supplement programs of study, the curriculum must include those prescribed by the government. Key Stages One and Two include the following subjects: religious education, English, mathematics, science and technology, history and geography (also referred to as the environment and society area of study), and art and design, music, and physical education (also referred to as the creative and expressive area of study) (CCEA 1999*a*).

At Key Stage Three the same subjects are included but students also begin the study of a modern language: Irish, French, German, Italian, or Spanish. At Key Stage Four the curriculum includes the same subjects as Key Stage Three with the addition of interdisciplinary themes that must be integrated into the other areas of study. These themes include the following, as titled by the CCEA: Education for Mutual Understanding, Cultural Heritage, Health Education, Information Technology, and Economic Awareness and Careers Education (CCEA 1999*b*).

Attainment targets and level descriptions. Attainment targets are achievement standards that define the expected level of pupil performance. Throughout the curriculum, attainment targets are expressed in terms of level descriptions that describe how a pupil should perform at any given stage. For example, there are eight levels in the curriculum; and at the end of Key Stage Three, a student should be performing at either Level Five or Level Six (CCEA 1999*b*).

Assessment. Assessment has been the main plank in the platform for education reform. The national curriculum prescribes assessment points and methods, with the stakes growing higher and higher as pupils progress through the key stages.

In Key Stage One and Key Stage Two, teachers conduct the assessments at the classroom level using assessment units that are prepared by the Council for the Curriculum, Examinations, and Assessment. Students do not actually take formal examinations, but the results of the teacher assessments are recorded on a uniform record of assessment that details how students have performed on the attainment targets and level descriptions that apply. It is not until the end of Key Stage Three that formal testing is part of the national assessment system (CCEA 1999*a*, 1999*b*).

At the end of Key Stage Three, students are assessed by teachers according to attainment targets and level descriptions; and they also sit for tests in English, Irish (if required by the school), mathematics, and science. Aggregate results of the tests are published in league tables, which follows practices in England and Wales (CCEA 1999*b*).

Transfer tests. Secondary Education in Northern Ireland is a two-track system, with about 40% of the students transferring at age 11 from primary school to the selective grammar schools. Grammar schools prepare students for admission to universities. The remainder transfer to secondary schools, which are non-selective (CCEA 1999*b*).

Students who plan to apply to one of the grammar schools take two tests in their last year of primary school, which is the sixth year of formal schooling. The tests cover subject matter from English and mathematics to science and technology. Students then are admitted to the grammar schools primarily on the basis of the grades on the transfer tests (CCEA 1999*c*).

Even though students who go to the non-selective secondary schools can still take the examinations for admission to universities (Northern Ireland uses the A-Level system, as do England and Wales), the system favors students who gain admission at age 11 to the grammar schools. The transfer testing system sorts out students at the point of transition between primary level and secondary level.

School environment. Although Northern Ireland's schools are segregated, they show consistency in their classroom environments. Physically the buildings and grounds are spare in comparison to a typical school in the United States. In addition, school, community, and classroom dynamics reveal a strong tradition of respect for the status of teacher. Like the classrooms in the neighboring nations of the United Kingdom and the Republic of Ireland, the primary schools typically are child-centered and the teaching methods normally are activity-based. More structure, both in the organization of subject matter and in the social system of the classroom, occurs at the secondary level, where teaching methods lean toward the didactic. In the primary schools the influence of Britain's emphasis on early childhood education is apparent, and in the secondary schools the importance of qualifying examinations is unmistakable.

Teacher Education

Teachers in primary or secondary schools must hold "qualified teacher status" from the Department for Education Northern Ireland (Fulton 1993, p. 229). However, formal teacher preparation is the responsibility of two universities and two colleges.

Public policy in teacher education has occupied considerable attention during the past quarter-century. And the issues are familiar to teacher educators elsewhere in the United Kingdom and in the United States. In the early 1970s the call for higher standards, as well as an oversupply of qualified teachers, led to consolidation of teacher training institutions. Throughout most of the 20th century, teacher preparation was accomplished through special institutions that offered only a teacher education curriculum. Indeed, in some cases the institutions were specialized for training teachers in specific disciplines, such as domestic science or physical education. A series of reports, particularly the Lockwood Report of 1965 and the Lelievre Report of 1973, resulted in the preparation of teachers being situated in comprehensive colleges and universities (Fulton 1993).

Today the structure of teacher education within the higher education environment is not appreciably different than in England or the United States. With the restructuring of institutions in place, officials in the Department for Education Northern Ireland and education faculties in higher education have turned their attention to the issue of balance between theory and practice. As in England and Wales, a strong movement is under way to make teacher education almost entirely school-based (Department for Education and Science 1991). Another contingent argues in favor of a more integrated approach that recognizes that there is a definitive body of knowledge in pedagogy that must be acquired in order to inform the professional development of the teacher. The debate continues as the colleges and universities that offer teacher preparation revise their programs in the wake of the Education Reform Order of 1989.

The Future of Education in Northern Ireland

"The management of the education system in Northern Ireland is in the process of upheaval." This rather blunt statement by Robert Osborne (1993, p. 9) understates the obvious. Since the creation of Northern Ireland's national system for education, controversy has been the norm. First came the question of whether the schools would be truly nondenominational, as the first Minister for Northern Ireland earnestly had hoped, or whether they would be Protestant. When Catholics opted out of state-controlled schools through the voluntary school scheme, the issue became moot. But then there was the matter of funding. In the 80 years of Northern Ireland's history, Catholic schools have gone from no funding to near parity. However, the gap did not close without acrimony. Today the implementation of reforms that have their origins in England has both the state-controlled schools (Protestant) and the voluntary maintained schools (Catholic) wary of what might come next. And if the shifting winds of education reform from England were not enough to make educators proceed with caution, the tentative status of Northern Ireland creates even more uncertainty. All that anyone knows for sure is that education policy now will begin taking its cues more from the politics of Belfast than from London. Indeed, the education system of Northern Ireland is in a perpetual state of change.

What can the people of the nation expect for their schools? What is their hope for their children? When you talk to parents and school children about their daily lives, you will hear them eager for a new beginning. Although no one expects the school system to desegregate in an instant, the surveys on school integration suggest a nation ready to begin the process of healing itself. In the meantime, members of Parliament will urge the nation to improve its global competitiveness and educators will implement the latest reforms handed down to them. But the real proof of change will come when there is equality of educational opportunity embedded both in the law and in the conscience of the nation.

CHAPTER FIVE

EDUCATION IN THE REPUBLIC OF IRELAND: NURTURING A NATIONAL IDENTITY
*by Sheryl O'Sullivan**

Ireland is a small country. It is about the size of Indiana, with a population of only 3.5 million people. It also is isolated, situated on an island on the very edge of European civilization and an ocean away from North America. Furthermore, Ireland has endured a history of invasions from foreign powers that interrupted and delayed Ireland's progress as a nation.

Despite the obstacles history and geography have placed in the way of its development as a nation, Ireland has gained the nickname, "Land of Scholars and Saints." It has given the world such literary figures as W.B. Yeats, James Joyce, Oscar Wilde, George Bernard Shaw, and John Synge. Cahill (1997), among others, credits Ireland with beginning the Renaissance in Europe by preserving and then disseminating literature that was lost during the Dark Ages on the continent. Ireland's education seems to have a long history of producing results. For such a small, remote, and oft-invaded country to effect such an early and sustained influence on world literacy is remarkable.

Historical Contexts

Our first real information about the place of education in Ireland comes from the Celts. This nomadic group of people probably arrived in Ireland about 300 B.C. Theirs was a tribal

---

*Sheryl O'Sullivan, Associate Professor of Education at Azusa Pacific University, kindly consented to provide this chapter on the Republic of Ireland's education system.

civilization with many different tribal chieftains and no unifying political power. But the civilization did have a common language, currency, and legal system.

In this culturally unified society, there were many different classes of freemen, and the uppermost layers were occupied by the most highly educated. Standing next to the tribal kings in Celtic society were the lawyers, the druids, and the poets. In order to become a druid, or Celtic priest, a man or woman had to study for at least 20 years. Poets were given places of honor in the Celtic court, and the power of their words was so great that to be cursed or shamed by a poet was enough to change the course of battles. Celtic heroes were required to become schooled in not only the arts of war, but also in poetry before they could assume their positions of leadership. With the Celts, the Irish devotion to learning had begun in earnest.

In the early 5th century a revolution of sorts came to Ireland in the form of Christianity. St. Patrick and other missionaries came to Ireland and found a society already primed to become a seat of learning. While the Celts had no written language to speak of, there was no shortage of educated people. Indeed, MacManus says of the time, "when Patrick came, in the early part of the fifth century, he found there such a plenitude of learning and learned men as necessitated a background of previous centuries of educational progress" (1999, p. 213).

Patrick found in Ireland not only the solid foundations of the druidic schools, but also a rural society that made it possible for the monastery, instead of the town, to become the center of learning. In addition, as Europe became increasingly hostile during the barbaric invasions, foreign students flocked to Ireland and mixed Latin, Greek, and the literary classics with the Gaelic language and indigenous tales and poems. Both monastic and lay schools were founded throughout the island during this time.

Most of the schools came into being because of the presence of a great teacher. A knowledgeable and skilled teacher would soon attract an ever-larger following of eager students. These students were instructed without fee but were obliged to care for the master's needs through old age. Students in these schools studied a wide variety of subjects: Gaelic literature, the scriptures, classical languages and literature, grammar, geography, history, law, mathematics, astronomy, philosophy, logic, rhetoric, music, art, and metal work (MacManus 1999). Irish, Latin, and Greek were the languages of instruction, and a 12-year course of study was necessary for anyone desiring to graduate with the highest rank. Schools such as these waxed during the early days of Christianity and waned during times of invasion, but they never died out entirely.

Ireland's devotion to education was sorely tested during the 18th and 19th centuries by a combination of harsh realities. First, England finally controlled Ireland through a mixture of military victories, colonizing plantations, and legal restrictions. The penal laws, passed in the early years of the 18th century, particularly singled out education as a means to oppress the population. For example, a Catholic was forbidden to receive an education, to educate his child himself, to send his child to a Catholic teacher, or to send his child abroad for an education (MacManus 1999). Since nearly all of the Irish were Catholic, these laws were specifically designed to reduce the Irish to ignorance. Instead, they brought about the birth of *hedge schools*. Returning to the early tradition of a master gathering informally with pupils, teachers met informally with small groups in hedgerows or other places that could conceal their activities. A poem titled "The Hedge Schoolmasters" attests to the bravery and necessity of the teachers in the hedge schools.

> When the night shall lift from Erin's hills, 'twere shame if
>   we forget
> One band of unsung heroes whom freedom owes a debt.
> When we brim high cups to brave ones then, their memory
>   let us pledge
> Who gathered their ragged classes behind a friendly hedge.
>   (MacManus 1999, p. 462)

The second harsh reality of recent times was the Irish famine, which lasted from 1845 to 1849 but left a profound influence on the land for much longer. While the penal laws and poverty had had some effect on Irish education — only 28% of the population was literate in 1844 — the famine was to have an even more devastating effect (Litton 1998). In the year before the famine began, Ireland had over eight million people, most of whom spoke Irish and practiced the Catholic faith. Within five years the population dwindled by approximately 2.5 million people. About 1.5 million of those died outright, and another million emigrated from Ireland.

English had largely supplanted the Irish language, and the old Gaelic traditions of hospitality toward poets and teachers were altered forever. Still, the devotion to learning was not entirely lost, as one Quaker relief worker observed. He remarked that he found it amazing to enter a house wracked with poverty and hunger to find quick-witted inhabitants still eager to engage in intellectual debate (Recorded in an exhibit, Irish Famine Museum, Dunfanaghy, Ireland).

By the early 20th century, Ireland at last began to recover from the combined effects of years of oppression and the devastating famine. The Gaelic League was founded to revive the traditional literature, language, and pastimes of old Ireland. With this came a new interest and pride in Irish nationalism. Schools such as St. Enda's, founded by Patrick Pearse, began to change the entire intellectual landscape of Ireland. In these schools, bilingualism was advocated and nearly all instruction took place in the Irish language. The heroic literature of Ireland was revived and taught alongside the classical literature of Europe. Music and drama were again made important parts of the curriculum, and everything was taught using the model of Jesus and Catholic Christianity as a guide. It was from these schools that much of the intellectual and sacrificial energy of the 1916 rising and subsequent War of Independence came. This War of Independence resulted in the political organization of Ireland that we know today. The lower 26 counties of Ireland are an independent country known as the Republic of Ireland, while the northern six counties are called Northern Ireland and remain a part of Great Britain.

This, then, is the historical context in which the schools of present-day Ireland find themselves. The schools in the Republic of Ireland have grown "organically," as one professor of education in Dublin put it. They have evolved over a long and complex past, always responding to the vagaries of the times and the needs of the population. Because of this complex past, schools in Ireland are not easy to describe, explain, or categorize. They defy glib simplification and require instead that any observer take into account the tenets of Irish society and the history within which Irish schools have evolved. Within these contexts the schools in the Republic of Ireland represent a very logical and systematic response to the current needs of a flourishing population.

Structure of the Schools

The organizational and governance structures of the schools of the Republic of Ireland today were defined and solidified through a series of activities immediately following Irish independence in 1921. However, as we have already seen, the current system of education has roots extending much farther into the past. A state-supported system of national primary schools was established throughout Ireland in 1831. Bilingual programs (Irish/English) were begun in 1904. And teacher training institutions received increased attention and importance so that, by 1900, 50% of all teachers had advanced training. All of these developments built on the earlier traditions of the hedge schools and provided a sound base for a system of education instituted around the time of independence and largely intact today (Coolahan 1981).

Shortly after the establishment of a free Ireland, several activities relating to education took place. These have proven to have far-reaching effects on education in the country today. In 1924 the Department of Education and Science formed. This department had regulatory powers over the curriculum, financing, and assessment of schools. It instituted broad curricular changes that narrowed and focused the existing curriculum and placed the Irish language in a position of increased importance in all schools. Compulsory attendance laws for six- to 14-year-olds came into effect in 1926. And intermediate and leaving certificate courses were established in 1924 for secondary schools. Clearly, education was to enjoy a place of importance in the newly formed Republic of Ireland.

Today the Irish education system is composed of three levels of schooling serving just fewer than one million students. First-level education consists of junior and senior infant groups and first through sixth classes. These schools are called primary schools, with all subsequent levels termed postprimary.

Second-level schools consist of three years of instruction leading to the Junior Certificate exam and a further two or three years of work that culminate in the Leaving Certificate exam. Second-level schools go by various names, such as secondary, vocational, comprehensive, or community schools or colleges. Third-level education consists of the universities, the technical institutes, and the colleges for the education of primary teachers.

First-level education (primary schools). Compulsory schooling does not begin in Ireland until age six, which is considered fairly late by international standards. However, this late compulsory age is largely moot, because early education is culturally accepted and valued in Ireland. Though it is not required that children begin school until they are six years old, according to the Irish Department of Education and Science (IDES 1998), 65% of all four-year-olds and virtually all five-year-olds are enrolled in junior or senior infant classes. Primary schools admit students beginning at age four and place students in one of the two infant classes or in first through sixth class. In the United States these classes would roughly correspond to prekindergarten, kindergarten, and grades one through six.

The primary portion of Irish education consists mainly of publicly funded primary or special schools, though there are a few non-aided private primary schools as well. Nearly 500,000 children attend primary schools, and they are taught by about 21,000 teachers. The schools continue to be small, with more than 50%

of all primary schools having four or fewer teachers. Ninety-eight percent of all primary students attend public schools, as there are only 64 private primary schools in the country. Preschool programs are provided by the state in a very limited way for three-year-olds with special needs. Older children with special needs are provided for in one of 116 publicly funded special schools (IDES 1998).

The philosophy of Irish primary education is child-centered. According to the Department of Education and Science:

> Primary education is founded on the belief that high-quality education enables children to realize their potential as individuals and to live their lives to the fullest capacity as is appropriate to their particular stage of development. (1998, p.12)

Today the national primary school system, which started in 1831, still serves as the most well-established piece of Irish schooling.

Second-level education. Schools for second-level education have a variety of names, including secondary, vocational, community, and comprehensive schools. These schools differ in governance and financial structures and in curricular emphases. The largest and most well-established type of school is the secondary school. Today 60% of all second-level students attend one of Ireland's 461 secondary schools. Vocational schools educate about 26% of the students in 248 schools, and another 14% of students are educated in 73 community or comprehensive schools (IDES 1998).

All second-level education includes a three-year junior cycle that leads to the completion of the Junior Certificate. After these three years, students may choose to advance directly to the two-year Leaving Certificate program or they may enter a transitional-year program designed to better prepare them for Leaving Certificate study. About 79% of all students now sit for one of three types of the Leaving Certificate exams available at the end of second-level instruction.

Attendance in second-level schools continues to rise in response to societal and legal changes. When compulsory schooling extended to only 14 years of age, only about 5% of Ireland's students attended second-level schools. The numbers increased gradually, but even in 1960 only 16% of students were attending second-level schools. This number increased dramatically in 1967 when secondary schools became free (Coolahan 1981). Today compulsory schooling extends to 16 years of age, and more than 370,000 students attend some type of second-level school. The goal is to have 90% of all students complete the senior cycle (IDES 1995).

Second-level students with special needs are served mainly by the ordinary secondary schools. While there are five second-level schools in Ireland designated as schools for physically, visually, or hearing impaired, these are not widely dispersed enough to serve the needs of the entire country. Instead, many regular secondary schools designate special classes for students with special needs. Some students are accommodated in regular schools with individualized learning programs similar to U.S. special education's "individualized education plan" (IEP).

Following 1967, when free second-level education was made available, many new second-level schools of all types were built to accommodate the increase in students. These schools tended to be larger than existing schools for both financial and curricular reasons. As a result, second-level schools shifted from being mostly below 500 students to mostly above. Today most schools serve between 300 and 700 students, with schools serving less than 100 students or more than 800 students being extremely rare (IDES 1995).

At the conclusion of second-level education, students attempt various further education programs. These opportunities for further education include vocational training, post-leaving-certificate courses, and apprenticeships, among others.

Third-level education (higher education). Third-level education in Ireland consists of the universities, the technological institutes, and the colleges of education. All of these enjoy substantial government funding. In addition, several private colleges recently opened offering mostly business-related courses of study. Attendance at third-level institutions has grown dramatically in recent years. Only about 18,500 students attended in 1965, while today there are more than 100,000 enrollees (IDES, n.d. *d*).

There are four universities in Ireland: the National University, the University of Dublin (Trinity College), the University of Limerick, and Dublin City University. The National University has four constituent campuses in Dublin, Cork, Galway, and Maynooth. These universities offer bachelor's, master's, and doctoral degrees in a variety of courses of study. Bachelor's degree programs are three or four years in length depending on the program.

For students who wish to follow a technological program, there are third-level institutions available throughout Ireland. The Dublin Institute of Technology enrolls more than 22,000 students, and a national system of technological institutes includes 12 regional sites throughout the country. Students in these programs can attain certificates, diplomas, or degrees, depending on their performance on examinations as regulated by the National Council for Educational Awards (IDES, n.d. *d*).

Finally, special colleges exist for the education of primary teachers. Currently there are five such facilities, four in Dublin and one in Limerick. Students who wish to be primary teachers complete a three-year course of study leading to a Bachelor of Education. Generally these colleges affiliate with one of the universities to confer degrees, but the colleges of education may also offer their own B.A. degree. In addition to these colleges for the education of primary teachers, there are five specialist colleges throughout Ireland to train secondary teachers in home economics, catechetics, and art. Other secondary teachers are trained at the universities.

Governance and finance. Nearly all of the primary and postprimary education in the Republic of Ireland is publicly funded. However, because virtually the entire population of Ireland is Christian, with 90% being Roman Catholic, the governance structures of these publicly funded schools are complex. In many

105

ways the entire school system of Ireland resembles the charter school system in the United States.

Nearly all public schools in Ireland are connected with a religious denomination, generally Roman Catholic. Most schools are affiliated with either a parish or a religious order. The supporting parish or order provides the buildings for the school and some continuing financial support. The state funds the current and capital expenses, including the cost of teacher's salaries. Primary schools are almost completely funded by the state, with second-level schools being funded between 93% and 95% of total costs. The remainder is provided through local sources. In addition, special funds are available for schools serving disadvantaged or special populations or that teach using the medium of the Irish language. Higher education is funded through the use of state grants. Students at all levels who attend state-aided schools are not charged tuition.

Local schools come under the direction of the board of management. This includes representation from teachers, parents, and the sponsoring agency, which is usually a parish or religious order. This local board or committee is responsible for the operation of the school, including the development of a comprehensive school plan. Therefore the school is under local control; however, it remains accountable nationally to the Department of Education and Science. This national government department issues the national curriculum, administers all national exams, and provides periodic inspections of all public schools. In addition, the department offers consulting services on a variety of topics, such as school planning and finance. It also engages with the legislature to promote legislation favorable to education. Local boards and committees establish the school ethos, but all public schools are responsible for teaching the approved national curriculum.

Curriculum and Assessment

Factors in modern Irish history such as the colonial past, the religious affiliations of the population, the cultural tradition of the people, the economic structure and the goals set

106

for education have all shaped the unusual, interesting and complex structure of the present-day Irish education system. (Coolahan 1981, p. 141)

As Coolahan so succinctly stated, the education system in place today in Ireland is a product of an intricate past. This is especially apparent in the curriculum and assessment of the schools. Building on the tradition of the hedge schools, Ireland has retained a respect for education, though the processes and desired products of education have undergone periodic revisions. An early attempt to standardize the curriculum and assess pupil achievement was the *Payment By Results* scheme in place from 1872-99. According to Coolahan (1981), this system of accountability for teachers encouraged a narrow and mechanical approach to teaching by prescribing precise programs and regular examinations. As the name implies, teachers were paid according to the results of pupil exams, leading to a lessened respect for teachers in general. Though this system was abandoned in 1899, the present-day schools continue to employ a national curriculum and state-controlled assessment.

Beginning about 1900 and continuing through the gaining of independence, Irish schools were called on to aid the nationalist movement by giving increased importance to the Irish language, history, and culture. While the specific national curriculum has undergone periodic revisions and the programs for student assessment have changed, the emphasis on national identity and pride remains a central feature of Irish schools.

Finally, there continues to be a noticeable difference in both curriculum and assessment between primary and postprimary schools. Postprimary schools are a relatively recent development for the general population. As recently as 1960, just before the implementation of free secondary schools, only about 16% of the students went on to postprimary education. Today, with compulsory attendance to age 16, all students progress to postprimary education; but the primary national schools still tend to be the backbone of the education system. Each of the two levels has specific curriculum and assessment in place that complements the other.

Primary curriculum and assessment. According to *Charting Our Education Future*, curriculum "encompasses the content, structure and processes of teaching and learning" (IDES 1995, p. 18). For the primary schools the curriculum was substantially revised in 1971 to a child-centered, rather than subject-centered, approach. This philosophy is still in place today, though the curriculum is currently under review.

The primary school curriculum is based on three principles. These include an emphasis on the whole child with attention paid to individual differences, the use of activity-based and guided-discovery teaching methods, and the integration of curriculum, especially focusing on the child's environment (IDES 1998). These principles continue to guide the curriculum even as portions of it are revised.

The revised curriculum includes a number of special emphases. One emphasis is literacy and numeracy. A fundamental aim of the curriculum is to ensure that students gain listening, speaking, reading, and writing literacy in their first language (National Council for Curriculum and Assessment 1997). For most students this is English. Further, all students must acquire basic numeracy and mathematical problem-solving skills.

The revised curriculum affirms the centrality of the arts within the schools and includes broad-based offerings in music, dance, drama, visual art, poetry, and storytelling. Study of the arts is considered to be a key way to assist children in becoming more tolerant, aware, and confident, nurturing creativity and artistic expression. The arts, therefore, are a particular aim of the primary curriculum.

Science plays an increasingly important role in the primary curriculum, and technology is particularly emphasized. Science has not been a focus of the curriculum in the past; but with technological advancements of present-day Ireland, the importance of the role of science is becoming increasingly recognized. The revised curriculum advocates the fostering of scientific thought processes and their application in other parts of the curriculum. Science within society and the environment is particularly emphasized.

The study of languages, especially the Irish language, has been an important part of the primary curriculum for nearly 100 years. The current revisions to the curriculum retain the centrality of the Irish language. Literacy in the child's first language is considered under the goals for literacy. For most children this is English; but for a minority, mostly children living in the Gaeltacht regions, first-language literacy is in Irish. For those students who do not have Irish as a first language, it is a compulsory subject throughout primary school. The goal of Irish-language instruction is for students to achieve conversational Irish by the end of primary school. Small pilot programs are now under way to introduce other European languages at the primary level. French, German, Italian, and Spanish are the targeted languages. Along with the study of languages, European life, art, and culture also are studied.

The revised primary curriculum also includes increased emphasis on physical education. Physical activity, health, and well-being are all components of the curriculum and extend to the school climate, parents, and the wider community, as well as to the students themselves. Personal identity, needs, and background are all considered within this curricular area.

Finally, the national schools continue to have the right to provide religious education according to the ethos of the school and community. Parents have the constitutional right to withdraw their children from religious education, but schools maintain the right and obligation to provide religious education that reflects the ethos of a majority of the parents and students. Families who do not subscribe to these beliefs are to be protected in a caring way, while not interfering with the instruction of the majority (National Council for Curriculum and Assessment 1999).

At the primary level there is no national system of exams or assessment. This is seen as both positive and negative. On the positive side, there are no high-stakes exams that could decide the course of a child's education too soon. Schools and teachers are in no danger of a return to the ill-conceived payment by results scheme. And no national network is needed to control and administer tests. On the negative side, however, there is general concern that some children are slipping through the cracks of education and that these underachievers may go unnoticed until external examinations begin at about age 15 (Coolahan 1994). Teachers do, of course, make use of a wide variety of tests within their classrooms. These include standardized tests, teacher-designed tests, work samples, portfolios, and observation. These are used for both diagnostic and evaluative purposes. At present, though, there is no agreement about if or how a national system of primary assessment should be established. This is seen as increasingly necessary if primary schools are to be given greater local control.

Secondary curriculum and assessment. Secondary curriculum consists of a junior cycle and a senior cycle with an optional transitional year between the two cycles. Both the junior and the senior cycles culminate with national examinations.

The Junior Certificate Programme was introduced in 1989 as a way to provide a unified course of study for students from approximately 12 to 15 years of age. Its principles include an emphasis on breadth and balance within the curriculum, relevance to immediate and future needs, attention to continuity and coherence, and an emphasis on excellence.

At the end of the junior cycle, students will achieve:

- Competence in literacy, numeracy, and spoken language.
- Experience in artistic, intellectual, scientific, physical, and practical activities.
- Formative moral, religious, and spiritual experiences.
- Knowledge in matters of personal health and well-being.
- Competence in practical skills, including information technology.
- Knowledge and appreciation of their heritage.
- Understanding of central concepts of citizenship (IDES 1995).

The program in the junior cycle consists of a core of Irish, English, mathematics, and a science or technological subject. Three other courses are chosen from a wide range of offerings, such as civic, social, and political education; the arts; religion and guidance; and physical education and health. The arts are considered a key element, and all schools should offer strong programs in the arts and cultural identity. In addition, all students should have access to the study of a modern European language.

The three years of study in the junior cycle culminate in the Junior Certificate examination. This is a nationally controlled and administered assessment and carries with it the special concerns of such tests. It can lead to a narrowing of curriculum and teaching methods and to the undervaluing of subjects not included on the test. However, this assessment is the first independent testing information available to students; and because the results of the Junior Certificate do not determine future education or career paths, the stakes are relatively low. After completing the Junior Certificate, students may choose to enter a transitional year or move immediately to a Leaving Certificate program.

The optional transition year has very specific goals that promote personal development and study skills before the student begins to study for a Leaving Certificate. The mission of the transition year is "to promote the personal, social, educational and vocational development of the students and to prepare them to participate as responsible members of society" (IDES, n.d. c, p. 3). The curriculum of the transition year is built around short units of study in more diverse areas than generally available. The year is designed to provide a bridge between the highly structured environment of the junior cycle years and the greater student responsibility necessary during the senior cycle. Interdisciplinary courses and a special emphasis on career exploration are key components of the transition-year program. These programs are optional, therefore students may elect to proceed directly from the junior cycle to a Leaving Certificate Program (IDES 1999). Students who are at least 16 years of age also may elect to leave school after completion of the junior cycle.

Senior cycle. Three types of Leaving Certificate programs are available for students, but no Leaving Certificate program can

111

extend past two years. The curriculum for the senior cycle focuses on the subjects needed for the Leaving Certificate examination. However, not all schools can offer every subject available on the exam. Therefore, the curriculum of all secondary schools is required to include study from an approved syllabus in the following areas:

- Irish
- English
- History and Geography
- Mathematics
- Science, or a language other than Irish and English, or a subject of the Business Studies Group
- Civic, Social, and Political Education (IDES 1999, p.7)

In addition, secondary schools must make provisions for instruction in relationships and sexuality, education, physical education, and singing. The rest of the secondary school curriculum focuses on additional Leaving Certificate options as deemed appropriate by the school. Vocational, comprehensive, and community schools generally would place more emphasis than secondary schools or colleges on vocational, technical, or applied topics.

Currently there are three different Leaving Certificate orientations from which students may choose. These are the established Leaving Certificate, the Leaving Certificate Vocational, and the Leaving Certificate Applied. All school curricula during the last two years of secondary school are focused on the successful completion of one of these three Leaving Certificates. There are 31 possible courses of study, which are selected in different ways according to the program being followed. The syllabi in these courses are standardized nationally by the National Council for Curriculum and Assessment.

The regular Leaving Certificate Programme is the most well-established of the three programs and serves as a base for the other two. The regular Leaving Certificate students choose five subject areas, of which one must be Irish. The approved subject areas are (IDES 1999, p.10):

Irish	Physics and Chemistry
English	Agricultural Science
Latin	Biology
Greek	Agricultural Economics
Classical Studies	Engineering
Hebrew Studies	Technical Drawing
French	Construction Studies
German	Home Economics (Scientific and
Italian	Social)
Spanish	Home Economics (General)
History	Accounting
Geography	Business
Mathematics	Economics
Applied Mathematics	Economic History
Physics	Art (including Crafts)
Chemistry	Music

All subjects are offered at two levels, higher and ordinary. Grades given at completion of the exam range from A, for 90% or better, to F, for less than 25% (IDES 1999). In addition to the regular levels of higher and ordinary, the subjects of Irish and Mathematics also are offered at a foundation level.

The Leaving Certificate Vocational Programme was introduced in 1989 and expanded in 1994 to allow a student to concentrate on technical subjects (IDES 1998). Five subjects are required, with two of these being chosen from a group of vocational subjects. The other three subjects must include Irish and a modern European language. In addition, students sitting for this exam must complete three link modules, which are short courses focusing on the world of work. Both the regular Leaving Certificate and the Leaving Certificate Vocational allow students to enter a variety of third-level education settings. The Vocational Certificate also enhances a student's preparation to enter directly into the world of work.

The Leaving Certificate Applied is the most recent of all the exams, with the first sitting held in 1997. This program was designed to meet the needs of students who were not being well served by the other two Leaving Certificates. It is a self-contained, two-year program of cross-curricular study with the primary objective of preparing students for adult and working life. There are three core areas in this program: vocational education, general education, and vocational preparation. Students spend 40% of their time in vocational education, 30% in general education, and 15% in vocational preparation. The remaining 15% of the time is discretionary. The Leaving Certificate Applied does not provide for entry into third-level education, but it does qualify a student for many Post-Leaving Certificate courses (IDES, n.d. *b*).

The present rate of completion for the senior cycle is 77%. But with the new and revised Leaving Certificate programs and the implementation of the transition year, a completion rate of 90% is expected in the near future. In 1997 more than 60,000 students took a Leaving Certificate exam. More than 2,000 superintendents and 2,800 examiners were needed to supervise and score these examinations. Scores on these exams are of key importance in acceptance to third-level and Post-Leaving Certificate programs; and the pressure is high for students, as it is with all high-stakes examinations (IDES 1997*b*).

The Teaching Profession

"If the mythical Martian were to arrive in the Republic of Ireland to investigate the dominant activity of its citizens, she or he might be forgiven for assuming that its principal industry is education" (Drudy and Lynch 1993, p. ix). Indeed, Department of Education statistics show that about one-third of the entire population of the country are full-time students at some level of schooling (IDES 1997*e*). Clearly teachers not only play a large role in education, but also are influential in the welfare of the country in general. Currently there are about 43,000 teachers at primary or second-level institutions. Most of these teachers teach at small schools. The majority, especially at the primary level, is female. And only about 4% to 6% of them are members of a religious order (IDES 1997*e*). Expenditures for these teachers account for more than 80% of the entire Department of Education budget (IDES 1995). It is clear that the quality of these teachers, and their continual support, is of vital interest and importance to the schools and to the country.

Ireland has had great respect for teachers dating back to the hedgerow master days and beyond. That respect largely continues today. Delegates at the National Education Convention, which brought together 42 different organizations concerned with education in Ireland, re-affirmed the "high valuation of the professional and caring tradition of the Irish teaching force" (Coolahan 1994, p. 85). Delegates at this convention also noted that historically Ireland has attracted many talented individuals to its teaching force and that it is vital for the high status of the teaching profession to be maintained in order to continue to attract people of high quality (Coolahan 1994).

One of the most important ways to maintain high quality and value in a profession is through a strong program of education and training that begins before the teacher is employed and continues throughout the teacher's years in service, with special attention paid to the crucial induction period at the beginning of a teacher's career. Ireland has such a program of strong preservice and inservice education for its teachers, though efforts are continually under way to improve this system. The education of primary teachers is especially strong, and there is good support for the continuation of this method of preservice education. Since the system of education for primary teachers is so different from that used for second-level teachers, each deserves an independent look.

Primary teachers. Most degree programs are three years in length. Students who wish to become primary teachers pursue a three-year Bachelor of Education (B.Ed.) degree at one of the country's special teacher training colleges. There are only five of these institutions, and four are in or near Dublin (IDES, n.d. *d*).

The entrance requirements for these colleges of education are quite stringent and available places are tightly controlled, so the prestige and integrity of the programs remain high. One of the most difficult entrance requirements is a proficiency in the Irish language. All students must study Irish throughout their careers, and so it is important that teachers are proficient in the language. This sometimes proves difficult for teachers moving to the Republic from Northern Ireland, and actions are under consideration that would allow an easier crossover between the two countries in this respect. However, commitment to the Irish language is strong; and teacher candidates must attend classes in a Gaeltacht (Irish-speaking) region as part of their first-year course of study (IDES 1997c).

The colleges of education employ a concurrent model of teacher education, which means that students pursue academic subject knowledge and pedagogical theory while concurrently practicing in primary classrooms. Many of the colleges of education affiliate with a university, where education theory courses are taught. Courses in the content of the curriculum and methods of teaching are taught at the college of education, which also supervises the classroom practice teaching. An example of this concurrent method of teacher preparation may be found at the Froebel College of Education in Blackrock, which is affiliated with Trinity College in Dublin. Students first enroll at Froebel College. In each of their three years, they take courses at Froebel in Irish, English, mathematics, art, music, religious studies, physical education, environmental studies, and the methods of teaching these subjects. Students attend Trinity one day per week for such courses as child development, history and philosophy of education, and statistics. There are six weeks of supervised practice teaching in local schools every year. At the end of three years, the successful candidate is awarded the B.Ed. degree and has the option of attending Trinity for one more year to follow an honors course leading to a Higher Diploma in Education.

There is good support for this method of concurrent preparation from the education community, largely because it works well.

Strong students are selected and given an integrated program in small, well-supervised cohort groups. While this preparation does not diminish the importance of careful induction and inservice opportunities, primary teachers are considered well-prepared to take their places as first-year teachers.

Second-level teachers. The concurrent training method is not widely used in the training of postprimary teachers. Only specialty teachers, such as those in home economics or physical education, use this method. Most students who wish to become secondary teachers pursue a three-year degree in one or more academic subjects and then take a one-year course leading to the Higher Diploma in Education. Again, there are only five institutions nationally that offer the Higher Diploma (H.Dip.); and four are not the same institutions that train primary teachers. Only St. Patricks College in Maynooth offers both programs for primary and second-level teachers.

The first three years of university study are no different for prospective teachers than for other students. During these years, the student completes the requirements for a degree in any academic subject area. The fourth year, in which the Higher Diploma in Education is pursued, is the year in which all pedagogical, theoretical, and practical education about teaching takes place. In that year, students take courses in methods, in education history and theory, and in adolescent development. At the same time, students spend several hours per week in second-level schools doing practice teaching. While the sponsoring university supports these students in many ways during their practice teaching, it does not arrange for their placement or supervision. Candidates find their own practice teaching situations, and this search is often as rigorous as any other job search (Guiry and Walker 1997).

The education community is less satisfied with the way in which second-level teachers are trained. Some needs cited by the Department of Education (IDES 1995) include better understanding of adolescent development, stronger knowledge of pedagogical and classroom management techniques, and more intentional mentoring of practice teaching activities. While the

H.Dip. programs vary widely across universities and revision of programs is constantly being undertaken, the Department of Education has requested that a systematic review take place of the education of second-level teachers.

Inservice education of teachers. Delegates at the National Education Convention in Dublin expressed wide support for the idea that the teaching career be viewed "as a continuum involving initial teacher education, induction processes and in-career development opportunities, available periodically throughout a teacher's career" (Coolahan 1994, p. 85). While this continuum is seen as an ideal, in Ireland it is not yet in place. The Department of Education is developing an induction-year program that would support new teachers as they attempt to apply the knowledge gained in preservice education through the use of mentors from both schools and teacher education institutes. This is as complex a task in Ireland as it is in the United States, and induction-year experiences vary markedly.

Still, inservice education in general is readily available. The Department of Education funds and monitors a huge program of inservice development. For example, in 1997 the department funded more than 200,000 inservice training days for teachers at primary and second levels. The department also funds the activities of 29 education centers throughout the country (IDES, n.d. *a*). These centers offer a variety of support services to teachers and administrators. For example, the Blackrock Education Centre in County Dublin offers inservice training for teachers in relationship and sexuality education, summer workshops in environmental education, and a support team for schools with the transition-year program (Blackrock Education Centre 1997).

While inservice education is widely available, there is a recognized need for better coordination of services that will support teachers throughout their careers. Especially as Ireland undergoes rapid educational and social changes, the needs of teachers for support can only intensify. The Department of Education has established priorities in inservice education around the areas of curricular revisions, including the integration of technology, students with special needs, fine arts, Irish and other languages, gender equality, collegiality, and adult literacy.

Teaching conditions. Teaching remains a valued career in Ireland. However, several conditions make it a relatively difficult lifestyle. Pay is not high. Primary teachers were paid the equivalent of between US$19,000 and US$37,000 in 1997. This was for a 183-day school year (IDES 1997c). Conditions among schools vary widely in terms of support for teachers. Many offer collegial, well-managed environments; but some are very difficult situations and offer little support. Finally, it is often difficult and time consuming for the new teacher to find a permanent position. Most first-year teachers enter the field in part-time, temporary, or substitute situations; and it often takes years to secure a permanent post. Despite these obstacles, idealistic and gifted young people still are enthusiastically entering the profession. As one young teacher, who had just received her first permanent post after seven years of teaching, writes, "It is almost a teacher's duty to remain starry-eyed about teaching — it is a wonderful and privileged job. . . . If you really truly burn to teach, go for it" (Guiry and Walker 1997, p. 16).

Trends and Issues in Irish Education

In the approximately 80 years that the Republic of Ireland has been an independent nation, education has grown and evolved and strengthened. The trends and issues that educators are facing today have many sources. Some, like the emphasis on Irish language and culture, are due to historical factors that left the Irish fervent about nurturing their national identity. Others, such as the inclusion of "traveller children," are in response to recent societal changes. Still others, such as the increased emphasis on technology, are the result of a vital and forward-thinking nation. In this section we will explore these three trends with a special view toward applying Irish insights to our own persistent education questions.

119

Bilingual education. Ireland's political history has led to the ironic fact that the official language of the country, which is Irish or Gaelige, is not the common language of the people, which is English. Due to a variety of political and social reasons, the Irish language was in deep decline at the beginning of the 20th century. The Gaelic League, which was formed at that time, had as its express purpose the revitalization of the Irish language and culture, and some schools were organized for this purpose. However, it remained for the new government of 1922 to solidify this goal into national education policy. They were quick to do this. Padraig O'Brolchain, the first chief executive officer for education, stated:

> In the administration of Irish education, it is the intention of the new government to work with all its might for the strengthening of the national fibre by giving the language, history, music and tradition of Ireland, their natural place in the life of Irish schools. (Coolahan 1981, p. 41)

Since 1922 bilingual education in some fashion has become the norm in Ireland. It usually takes one of three forms. First, there are Irish-speaking schools within the Gaeltacht regions of Ireland. The 85,000 people who live in these regions still have Irish as their mother tongue and use it in their daily lives. Students who attend Irish-speaking schools in these regions are learning all subjects, except English, in their first language.

Second, students in the rest of the country generally have English as their first language but have the option, in many areas, of attending Irish-only schools. The Gaelscoileanna are immersion schools that teach all the normal primary or secondary curricula using the Irish language. Young students enter from an English-speaking world with virtually no background in Irish. Most will speak Irish fairly well by the end of the first year and proficiently by the end of the second. Many primary Gaelscoil students go on to secondary Irish-language schools, but many also enter English-language secondary schools without difficulty. The government encourages the establishment of Gaelscoileanna through favorable funding schemes, and there has been a steady growth in these types of schools in recent years. In 1997 there were 112 primary and 24 second-level Irish-language schools in the country. These schools served more than 22,000 students and employed approximately 1,100 full-time teachers (Gaelscoileanna 1998). Though little research on the subject of bilingual education is conducted in Ireland, students in the Gaelscoileanna do well at all levels of education in both Irish and English. In fact, the results of a study of trilingual students in Ireland suggest that instead of being a burden on learners, one or more additional languages are actually beneficial for student achievement (Ni Chleirigh 1990).

Finally, students from English-speaking households may attend English-speaking schools and learn most of their subjects in their first language. However, all students are required to take Irish every year as a second language, and Irish is included as a subject on the Leaving Certificate and is required for admission to teacher training programs. In addition, most public signs and documents are written in both Irish and English, and there are Irish-language radio and television stations so that all students have at least some association with Irish in their daily lives. The students in the English-speaking schools achieve varying levels of proficiency with Irish, as may be expected. However, even with varying levels of success, our own bilingual programs might benefit from the examination of a program of bilingual education that has been so positively integrated into mainstream education.

Travellers. Much of Irish education policy has focused on the reawakening and redefining of a national identity, yet there is a real sense of the responsibilities of education as well. This stance is very evident in the current emphasis on better meeting the needs of transient students, called "traveller children."

Travellers in Ireland are extremely mobile groups of people, such as circus workers, gypsies, and seasonal workers. They live in caravans beside the roads and come and go as they wish, depending on a variety of circumstances. Their children experience numerous difficulties with school settings. Their culture emphasizes different values from the settled communities, and school attendance can be very sporadic. The children sometimes are ostracized because of their differences, and they often receive little encouragement at home to continue with schooling. Historically very few traveller children continued into second-level education, and even today only about 5% of eligible students are attending any sort of second-level school (O'Brien 1997).

While there are many reasons why traveller children do not experience success in school, there are concerted efforts in Ireland today to improve the success rate of these students. The many suggestions for facilitating schooling for travellers include:

- Helping teachers deal with students of different backgrounds and including these children in the classroom without over-emphasizing their differences.
- Using innovative teaching methods and materials.
- Raising awareness that these children are generally the first generation in the family to attend school regularly and the home will not be well able to support them.
- Recognizing that community and personal stereotypes of these children are often negative and must be countered with success (McDonagh 1997).

The Department of Education and Science has included policy statements for the education of travellers in its *White Paper on Education* (IDES 1995). The overall goal of the department is to increase the number of traveller children in the successful education community. To that end, all schools must include provisions for travellers in their school plans. A visiting teacher service is funded by the department to act as a liaison between the settled and traveller communities. The curriculum of schools is adapted to the special needs of these students and includes modules for teachers on the traveller culture. The programs for travellers and their attendance patterns are regularly monitored and evaluated by the department. At second level, special classes and Junior Training Centres are used as a bridge to integrate traveller students into regular classrooms. With these efforts, Ireland hopes to soon have all primary traveller children enrolled in school and to see 50% of these students complete the senior cycle. While these are very ambitious goals, the emphases of these initiatives on inclusion and anti-racism are to be commended.

Technology. Perhaps it is not surprising, given the relatively brief amount of time that Ireland has been an independent and increasingly prosperous country, that it should lag behind other European Union countries in the integration of computers into education. However, as the country becomes more prosperous, it is able to look forward and prepare for life in the information age. In order to ensure that its students are prepared in information and communication technologies, the Department of Education and Science has launched a major campaign titled "Schools IT 2000" (IDES 1997*d*).

This initiative, which began in 1997 and continues through 2001, is designed to ensure that every student has the opportunity to achieve computer literacy and that teachers are able to develop new skills around information and communication technologies. To that end, the government is investing the equivalent of about US$36 million and is pursuing partnerships with businesses, such as the recent Telecom Eireann investment of the equivalent of US$14 million in the project.

The project strategies are clustered around three areas: technology infrastructure, skills infrastructure, and support infrastructure. At least 60,000 multimedia computers will be placed in schools by 2001, and every school will be connected to the Internet. In order to ensure the skills necessary to use these computers, at least 20,000 teachers will have special inservice programs, while preservice teachers will have information and communication skills built into their initial education. In addition, distance learning will be used for ongoing training. Finally, support for this initiative will come through curricular changes, the establishment of a national advice network called Scoilnet, and the creation of appropriate curriculum resources.

While achieving the integration of information and communication technologies in all Irish classrooms is a daunting task, many agencies and constituencies are committed to this goal because of its social, vocational, economic, and pedagogic benefits. If the aims of "Schools IT 2000" are reached, it will be because a national strategic plan was developed, funded, and followed. Such an organized and single-minded approach could serve as a model for other programs wishing to make noticeable improvement in the integration of technology in the classroom.

Summary

Ireland's education system has grown naturalistically into its current state in response to the changing needs of society. It evolved historically using the very prominent role of the Catholic Church and the very certain determination of the Irish people to re-establish their cultural identity after gaining independence from Britain. While the Irish system resembles both the American and the British systems in many ways, it also has substantial systemic and philosophic differences. The entire system, while very complex and creative, is well-ordered and successful. Irish education has responded well to the intricacies and demands of Irish society.

In order to continue to be successful, Irish schools will need to continue to respond creatively to changes in Ireland. The changes on the horizon include increased participation in second- and third-level courses, a declining birth rate, a decline in religious vocations, an increase in parental and business influence in the schools, and a greater emphasis on international perspectives (Coolahan 1994). These and other trends could change the face of Irish schools in the near future and must be embraced as challenges before they become crises.

Irish education will continue to evolve in a positive way. The students are well-motivated and are raised in a society that values education. The teachers are well-educated and operating in a work environment that generally values their contributions. The schools have a complex balance of academic, spiritual, and artistic goals, which include both personal growth and social responsibilities. Though maintenance of a strong school system is never an easy task, the Irish have a firm foundation on which to build their future.

CHAPTER SIX

THEMES IN BRITISH AND IRISH EDUCATION

Shakespeare wrote, "Comparisons are odorous" (*Much Ado About Nothing*, III, v). But his admonition has never stopped us from making them. We have the tendency to define ourselves by how we compare in relation to others, both individually and nationally. Sometimes these comparisons can result in anxiety and self-deprecation. At other times they can be the basis for pointless boasting. But they also can stimulate healthy self-assessment and lead to a better understanding of ourselves. This last result is the reason for comparative education.

To make a comparison between U.S. education and British and Irish education, we may ask such questions as: What can we observe that has relevance to our own system and our desire to improve? How can educators in the United States learn from agendas for education reform in Great Britain and Ireland? How do they deal with the same issues, the same persistent problems, the same uncertainties about a future in a world that is at the same time increasingly competitive and increasingly interdependent? Several themes that run through British and Irish education might tell us how they handle these questions.

England and Wales

Several questions persist in the British national dialogue on school reform. How do we get children ready to learn? What do we do with children whose native language is not English? Should we have a national curriculum and national assessment? How do we best prepare prospective teachers? British answers to questions facing educators in the United States are not likely to produce panaceas, but they will help enlarge the range of options when considering solutions. Experience is the best teacher, even if it has been someone else's experience.

Emphasis on early childhood education. Great Britain has embraced early childhood education as an integral part of the primary education system. Not only do children begin their formal education earlier in Britain than in the United States, the practices adhere more closely to developmental theory. Social skills are taught in a naturalistic environment, and language enrichment is the focus for the curriculum. Given the extraordinary ease with which children in Britain move into the early stage of primary school, both socially and educationally, states in America would do well to consider lowering the beginning age for compulsory education from six to five. In addition, voluntary enrollment for three- and four-year-olds could be supported by the state. Britain, as well as most nations in Europe, has demonstrated that the policy is economically feasible.

Bilingual education. In the case of bilingual education, Wales is the best example in Great Britain. The only indigenous bilingual population in Britain lives in Wales, and the Welsh have clung to their language as a matter of cultural pride. Children grow up speaking both Welsh and English, and formal instruction in both languages begins at once in the school.

While bilingual education in Wales seems to be a model of cultural harmony, the case really misses the point when applied to children who come to school never having spoken English. Schools in the ethnic ghettos of London face the same dilemmas as schools in the bilingual communities of the United States, and the British solutions have been no more effective. Immersion ESL programs and concurrent bilingual education programs both are tried, and critics can be found for either approach. The national curriculum is explicit — proficiency in the English language is required on the qualifying examinations. So far, however, the record of achievement on these examinations by immigrant children suggests Britain is still looking for policies and programs that will work for its rapidly changing society.

National curriculum and accountability. The national curriculum and national qualifying examinations for leaving secondary school are the heart of education reform in Britain. In this respect government policy on education reform is remarkably different. In Britain, the national government sets the education standards and the school determines the best way to enable students to reach those standards. A secondary school principal in Banbury, England, said it succinctly:

> The government doesn't care how much time my students spend on a subject or how we teach . . . we can play football all day for all they care, as long as my students pass their A-levels. (Green 1996)

Perhaps by following the British example, American government agencies could worry less about prescribing phonics-only textbooks or dictating block scheduling and focus on the accountability of schools for student performance. In British education, the intended outcome is described in great detail, but the method is left to local school authorities and teachers.

Teacher education. In the professional preparation of teachers, Britain has experienced many of the same shock waves of reform that have occurred in the United States. Disenchantment with teacher education programs in the polytechnic colleges and universities led to sweeping changes. Teacher education programs in universities now are more school-based, and practicing educators are more directly involved. Also, the induction of beginning teachers is given high priority. Of course, this trend parallels the improvements seen in American teacher education. In Britain it is understood that anyone qualified to teach a subject at the secondary level should have a university degree in that subject. "Emergency" credentials are not issued in the same wholesale fashion as found in some states in America. Again the influence of the national examinations is a factor. In a subject-centered curriculum with a national examination system, the subject matter preparation of the teacher is essential. This uncompromising stand on the academic qualifications of teachers is worth noting by any education policy maker in the United States. Whether England and Wales can continue this policy is a critical question, now that shortages of teachers in mathematics, science, and technology are beginning to occur.

School choice. In the United States school choice had been a focal point of the debate on education reform. In England and Wales it is taken for granted. Not only can parents choose the school where their children will attend, as a community, parents can choose whether their school will remain under the control of the local education authority (LEA). A central feature of education reform in England and Wales is the "grant-maintained school" status, which allows a school to receive its funding directly from the national government and create its own governing board. A school community has the option to choose the kind of governance structure it will have, and parents have the option to choose individual schools. While not the panacea that school choice advocates in the United States promise, a national policy of school choice and alternative structures for school governance have served the purpose of dislodging the local education authority as the predominant power in education. LEAs now must be responsive, rather than resistant, to the demands for change in education.

Scotland

The distinguishing characteristic of Scottish education is local autonomy. While the education reform initiatives of the last decade have resulted in new versions of the national curriculum and its assessment system, both are advisory, rather than mandatory. In effect the government of Scotland has accepted the role of leading education reform, rather than dictating it. This approach to reform — leading rather than pushing — is almost unknown to educators in America, who are reeling from top-down micro-management from state departments of education and the federal government.

Education policy in Scotland grows from a process of consensus building that includes all constituent groups — teachers, administrators, parents, unions, government officials, as well as business and industry. No one group has the upper hand, and each group relies on the support of the others. Agendas defined by partisan politics are conspicuously absent. Why? Certainly the small scale of the system in comparison to the United States or England is a factor. Also, the homogeneity of the population helps in focusing the issues. But in addition to these factors, the Scottish education system enjoys relative equanimity because the teaching profession is respected and the contribution of teachers to the democratic process of local control of schools is valued.

Scots have a penchant for order and efficiency but disdain for impersonal bureaucracy. In a pragmatic fashion, they expect their institutions to work. Perhaps that explains why so much responsibility in education rests with local political subdivisions and individual schools, rather than with the central government. Also, it may explain why schools are characteristically smaller than those found in either the United States or England. With sharply focused goals and locally defined terms of accountability for reaching those goals, schools do not have to be all things to all people. Nor do they require bureaucracies to manage complex arrays of functions.

The Scottish system of education is centered on the essential purposes of education, and its teaching profession is expected to provide leadership at both the local and national levels.

Northern Ireland

At present, the education system in Northern Ireland is attempting to repair itself after decades of religious segregation. The question that eventually dominates any discussion of the country's education future is whether that repair is possible. Does integration really have a chance of succeeding? Can there be equality of opportunity as long as there are separate school systems for Protestants and Catholics? Can a nation expect to heal itself of religious prejudice as long as it remains divided in the very place where its children learn their places in society? If any nation ever needed a case study in the long-term effects of inequalities born of segregation, Northern Ireland would provide the grist.

Abraham Lincoln, writing during America's Civil War, observed, "We cannot escape history." The occasion was his annual address to Congress, and he was exhorting the country's leaders to honorable behavior during the young nation's greatest crisis. A parallel to Northern Ireland can be drawn. It, too, cannot escape its history. And if its history is to become one of Protestants and Catholics finally learning to live in peace and harmony, then the schools will have played a vital role. Similarly, if its history is to become one of continued civil war, then the schools also will have played a role. Either way, the education system of Northern Ireland at the turn of the 21st century will play a part in making history.

Republic of Ireland

Schooling in the Republic of Ireland resembles education in the United Kingdom in many ways. Indeed, Irish schools were organized around the English education system during a time in history when Ireland was a part of England. It is not surprising, then, that Irish schools share with the United Kingdom such attributes as small size, an emphasis on parental choice, and a philosophy of national standards with local control. Even with these similarities, however, Irish schools maintain a distinctly Irish flavor; and these distinctive characteristics could offer us ideas on ways to embrace school reform in the United States. A look at Irish schools offers four basic areas that could benefit Americans.

First, the entire country seems to follow a charter-school mentality. This has several benefits. Parents and the local community play a primary part in the education system. Parents can choose where to send their children to school and what type of school suits them best. They even can begin a new school with state support if the available schools are inadequate. This results in schools that suit the needs of and are accountable to the local community. Since all schools are responsive to the needs and desires of the people who will use them, each school has a distinctive ethos, which is acceptable and successful. The state does not designate or control what this individual ethos will be beyond requiring a national curriculum. The result of the whole system is that state, church, community, and parents all work together in ways that benefit each constituency. The distinctions between public and private, religious and secular, and state and local control are blurred in ways we in the United States would consider unacceptable. However, in Ireland the blurring of all these divisions has resulted in cohesive, integrated, and successful schools without the dissention found around these issues in our own schools.

Second, Ireland's commitment to bilingual education could serve as a model for our own efforts in this area. The preservation of the Irish language is a matter of national pride, and this attitude alone represents a very different philosophy from the apparent American philosophy that all languages except English are to be discouraged. Since Irish is a second language, but treasured, the schools provide multiple levels of support for learning language, which schools in the United States have been unwilling to provide. And this support is largely compatible with research on best practices in bilingual education. Students with Irish as a first language are taught in this language before beginning English. Students whose first language is English have the option of entering full-immersion Irish schools or taking Irish as a required subject in English-speaking schools. The curriculum in Irish begins in primary school and continues in a cohesive way through secondary school to a required component on the leaving certificate. Irish-language materials and special funding are available from the state to encourage and support the teaching of Irish. How much better might our own bilingual programs be with similar philosophical, curricular, and monetary support?

Third, teacher education for primary teachers in Ireland could serve as a model for us as we continuously re-assess our own teacher education programs. Admissions standards are higher than general college acceptance standards, and curriculum is focused on increasing subject matter competency. However, this increased content knowledge is integrated continuously every year with increasing pedagogical skills. Students study content, methods, and children all at once, in coursework and actual practice, throughout their entire program. No division exists between subject matter preparation and teacher preparation. The organization of the Irish primary teacher education means that entering students take part in a cohesive and challenging curriculum that results in a well-prepared, committed, and respected teaching force. The Irish habit of charter schools continues into teacher education so that religious and secular schools cooperate easily to provide different pieces of teacher training. This avoids the circumstance often found in the United States in which the competing demands of state regulations, university requirements, and local needs result in a bloated, disjointed, and often unsuccessful program of teacher training.

Finally, Ireland has great respect for the arts, and this respect is displayed in the Irish curriculum. A school principal in Ranelagh, when questioned on which subjects were most important in school, listed reading, mathematics, and music as the top three subjects. The arts, particularly music, are given a place of prominence in the national curriculum and are viewed as a way to help students become more human. Music, drama, and dance are encouraged by the culture and supported in the schools. Far from being the first-to-go frills we seem to consider them in the United States, the arts are an integral part of the Irish curriculum.

There are so many superficial and profound ways in which Irish culture and schooling differ from American culture and schooling that to suppose we could simply graft the Irish way onto our systems would be foolhardy. Still, even with the limitations of our differences, many of the ways in which Ireland has gone about schooling its children could be applicable to us. Curricular emphases in the arts and bilingual education, a strong program of primary teacher education, and a national system that includes respect for local control are all areas that could be useful in our own struggles with school reform.

Summary

The British and Irish education systems are products of their unique histories and evolving national agendas. And each reflects its particular cultural heritage. However, several themes are shared in common. When we examine the recent developments of education reform, these themes make a sharp contrast to education policy in the United States.

First, all nations emphasize a national curriculum and a national system for assessment. Certainly the geographic compactness of the nations, as well as cultural homogeneity, contributes to the public's general agreement on this issue. Even so, in comparison to the United States, policy makers and school patrons do not view the issue of accountability as controversial. While there are voices of dissent, they serve more to keep the system responsive than to paralyze the process of change.

Similarly, the question of school choice never has been an issue in the formulation of education reform policy in the United Kingdom and Ireland. The question always has been how to facilitate choice and expand the options of students and parents. The notion of a school having a monopoly defined by an attendance area is puzzling to the British and Irish. As one Irish principal put it, "Why would you want to do that?"

The physical appearance of British and Irish schools is in stark contrast to American schools. They are smaller, and they are more modest in both design and furnishings. Typical elementary enrollments of 200 to 400 and secondary school enrollments of 600 to 800 pupils indicate that neighborhood schooling is alive and well in Great Britain and Ireland. Moreover, the governance structures give considerable authority to councils at the school level for operations.

Another very significant feature of education in Great Britain and Ireland is the emphasis on early childhood education. Formal education begins at age five, and more than half the four-year-olds attend preschool. Educators and policy makers uniformly appreciate the importance of high-quality early childhood education, and a key feature of education reform policy has been to expand access to preschool programs.

Nurturing cultural and linguistic identity is an explicit aspect of national curricula. The Republic of Ireland includes the study of Irish alongside the study of English, and the number of Irish immersion schools — Gaelscoileanna — is increasing. In Wales, students also study the language of their cultural heritage, Welsh, alongside English. In these countries, bilingual education is viewed as a strategy to nurture a heritage in addition to preparing students for modern society. The question is not, How do we make English the only language? Rather, it is, How do we keep our heritage alive and also equip our students with the language skills to be successful in national and international commerce?

Finally, in the Republic of Ireland and Scotland the profession of teaching is highly respected. Although the financial compensation does not compare to other professions requiring comparable higher education, teachers are held in high esteem in the community. Indeed, a recent public opinion poll in Ireland revealed that teachers ranked just below nurses and physicians (general practitioners) in terms of public esteem. Teachers ranked ahead of pharmacists, dentists, lawyers, and business managers (ASTIR 1998). As a consequence, the professional opinions of teachers count in the public process of policy development. Similarly, in Ireland or Scotland, teacher education has not become the national scapegoat that it has in the United States or in England and Wales. While teachers and teacher educators in Scotland and Ireland acknowledge that improvement is needed, especially in secondary teacher education and inservice education, they do not have to brace themselves against steady assault. Rather, they are able to harness their energy in collaboration with national agencies. Scotland and the Republic of Ireland offer mutual respect and cooperation with their educators.

In conclusion, can we judge the schools of the United Kingdom or the Republic of Ireland as any better than those in the United

States? Or can we justify any claim that U.S. schools are superior? I believe the answer to both questions is "No." We can only observe where the systems are similar and where they are different. And, more important, we can observe how the course of history and the drive of culture have accounted for those differences. The purpose is neither the national self-aggrandizement nor the national self-deprecation that results from rankings. Either paralyzes attempts at the meaningful reform of a system of education, just as either will stunt individual personal development. Rather, we learn about other systems of education so that we might gain a broader perspective for understanding our own — a perspective that allows us to extend our vision of the horizon that defines the possibilities for our schools.

REFERENCES

Akenson, D.H. *The Irish Education Experiment: The National System of Education in the Nineteenth Century*. London: Routledge, 1970.

Association of Secondary Teacher Ireland (ASTIR). "Teachers Held in High Esteem." *ASTIR* (May 1998): 4.

Atkin, J.M., and Black, P. "Policy Perils of International Comparisons." *Phi Delta Kappan* 79 (September 1997): 22-28.

Berliner, D.C., and Biddle, B.J. *The Manufactured Crisis: Myths, Fraud, and the Attack on America's Public Schools*. New York: Longman, 1997.

Blackrock Education Centre. *Official Opening*. Dun Laoghaire, Eire, 1997.

Cahill, T. *How the Irish Saved Civilization*. New York: Bantam Doubleday Dell, 1997.

Cairns, E.; Dunn, S.; and Giles, M. "Surveys of Integrated Education in Northern Ireland: A Review." In *After the Reforms: Education and Policy in Northern Ireland*, edited by R.D. Osborne et al. Aldershot, U.K.: Avebury, 1993.

Central Statistical Office (CSO). *Annual Abstract of Statistics, No. 130*. London: Her Majesty's Stationery Office, 1994. a

Central Statistical Office (CSO). *Social Trends, No. 24*. London: Her Majesty's Stationery Office, 1994. b

Chartered Institute of Public Finance and Accountancy (CIPFA). *Local Government Trends 1990*. London, 1991.

Chartered Institute of Public Finance and Accountancy (CIPFA). *Education Statistics: 1991-92 Actuals, Incorporating the Handbook of Education Unit Costs*. London, 1993.

Clark, K. *Civilisation*. New York: Harper & Row, 1969.

Clark, M.M. "Education in Scotland: Setting the Scene." In *Education in Scotland: Policy and Practice from Pre-School to Secondary*, edited by M.M. Clark and P. Munn. London: Routledge, 1997. a

Clark, M.M. "Developments in Primary Education." In *Education in Scotland: Policy and Practice from Pre-School to Secondary*, edited by M.M. Clark and P. Munn. London: Routledge, 1997. b

Clark, M.M. "The Teaching Profession: Its Qualifications and Status." In *Education in Scotland: Policy and Practice from Pre-School to Secondary*, edited by M.M. Clark and P. Munn. London: Routledge, 1997. c

Closs, A. "Special Education Provision." In *Education in Scotland: Policy and Practice from Pre-School to Secondary*, edited by M.M. Clark and P. Munn. London: Routledge, 1997.

Coolahan, J. *Irish Education: History and Structure*. Dublin: Institute of Public Administration, 1981.

Coolahan, J. *Report on the National Education Convention*. Dublin: National Education Convention Secretariat, 1994.

Cormack, R.J.; Gallagher, A.M.; and Osborne, R.D. *Religious Affiliation and Educational Attainment in Northern Ireland: The Financing of School in Northern Ireland, Standing Advisory Committee on Human Rights, Report for 1990-1991*. London: Her Majesty's Stationery Office, 1991.

Council for the Curriculum, Examinations, and Assessment (CCEA). *Primary Curriculum and Assessment*. 1999. a. Available at www.ccea.org.uk.

Council for the Curriculum, Examinations and Assessment (CCEA). *Post-Primary Curriculum and Assessment*. 1999. b. Available at www.ccea.org.uk.

Council for the Curriculum, Examinations and Assessment (CCEA). *Post 16 Qualifications*. 1999. c. Available at www.ccea.org.uk.

Dearing, R. *The National Curriculum and Its Assessment: Final Report*. London: School Curriculum and Assessment Authority, 1993.

Department for Education (DFE). *Statistics of Schools 1992*. London: Her Majesty's Stationery Office, 1993. a.

Department for Education (DFE). *Statistics of Education: Public Examinations: GCSE and GCE, 1992*. London: Her Majesty's Stationery Office, 1993. b

Department for Education (DFE). *Statistical Bulletin 16/93: Participation in Education by 16-18-Year-Olds in England, 1979/80 to 1992/93*. London, 1993. c

Department for Education (DFE). *School Teachers' Pay and Conditions Document 1994*. London: Her Majesty's Stationery Office, 1994.

Department for Education and Office for Standards in Education. *Department Report: The Government's Expenditure Plans, 1994-95 to 1996-97*. London: Her Majesty's Stationery Office, 1994.

Department for Education and Science. *Special Education Needs: Report of the Committee of Enquiry into the Education of Handicapped Children and Young People*. London: Her Majesty's Stationery Office, 1978.

Department for Education and Science. *School-Based Initial Teacher Training in England and Wales: A Report by Her Majesty's Inspectorate*. London: Her Majesty's Stationery Office, 1991.

Department of the Environment. *Annual Report 1994: The Government's Expenditure Plans, 1994-95 to 1996-97*. London: Her Majesty's Stationery Office, 1994.

Drudy, S., and Lynch, K. *Schools and Society in Ireland*. Dublin: Gill & MacMillan, 1993.

Dunn, S. "A Historical Context to Education and Church-State Relations in Northern Ireland." In *After the Reforms: Education and Policy in Northern Ireland*, edited by R.D. Osborne et al. Aldershot, U.K.: Avebury, 1993.

Elley, W.B. *How in the World Do Students Read?* Hamburg: International Association for the Evaluation of Educational Achievement, 1992.

Fulton, S. "Teacher Education: Some Policy Considerations." In *After the Reforms: Education and Policy in Northern Ireland*, edited by R.D. Osborne et al. Aldershot, U.K.: Avebury, 1993.

Gaelscoileanna. *All Irish-Education Outside the Gaeltacht, 1997/98*. Dublin, 1998.

Green, J.E. Unpublished raw data from interviews of selected British educators, 1996.

Green, J.E. Unpublished data from interviews of selected British and Irish educators, March 1998 and June 1998.

Guiry, E., and Walker, S. *Graduate Careers in Teaching and Education*. Dublin: Association of Graduate Careers Services in Ireland, 1997.

Gutek, G. *American Education in a Global Society: Internationalizing Teacher Education*. New York: Longman, 1993.

Harrison, C. "How Scottish is the Scottish Curriculum: And Does It Matter?" In *Education in Scotland: Policy and Practice from Pre-School to Secondary*, edited by M.M. Clark and P. Munn. London: Routledge, 1997.

Her Majesty's Inspectorate. *Scottish Schools: Costs 1993/94 to 1995/96*. Edinburgh: Audit Unit, Scottish Office Education and Industry Department, 1996.

Hlebwitsh, P., and Tellez, K. *American Education: Purpose and Promise*. Belmont, Calif.: Wadsworth, 1997.

Irish Department of Education and Science (IDES). *Charting Our Education Future: White Paper on Education*. Dublin, 1995.

Irish Department of Education and Science (IDES). *Key Education Statistics: 1985/86 to 1995/96*. Dublin, 1997. a

Irish Department of Education and Science (IDES). *Leaving Certificate Examination*. Dublin, 1997. b

Irish Department of Education and Science (IDES). *Primary Teacher Training in Colleges of Education*. Dublin, 1997. c

Irish Department of Education and Science (IDES). *Schools IT 2000*. Dublin, 1997. d

Irish Department of Education and Science (IDES). *Statistical Report*. Dublin, 1997. e

Irish Department of Education and Science (IDES). *A Brief Description of the Irish Education System*. Dublin, 1998.

Irish Department of Education and Science (IDES). *Rules and Programme for Secondary Schools, 1999/00*. Dublin, 1999.

Irish Department of Education and Science (IDES). *Customer Service Statement*. Dublin, n.d. a

Irish Department of Education and Science (IDES). *The Right Track: The New Senior Cycle*. Dublin, n.d. b

Irish Department of Education and Science (IDES). *Senior Cycle: The Restructured Curriculum*. Dublin, n.d. c

Irish Department of Education and Science (IDES). *Third-Level Education in Ireland*. Dublin, n.d. d

Litton, H. *The Irish Famine*. Dublin: Wolfhound Press, 1998.

Locke, T.; Cavendish, R.; and Rogerson, B. *Exploring Britain*. New York: Fodor's Travel, 1996.

Mackinnon, D.; Stratham, J.; and Hales, M. *Education in the UK: Facts and Figures*. London: Hodder and Stoughton, 1995.

MacManus, S. *The Story of the Irish Race*. New York: Barnes & Noble, 1999.

Maeroff, G. "Focusing on Urban Education in Britain." *Phi Delta Kappan* 73 (January 1992): 352-58.

McAdams, R.P. *Lessons from Abroad: How Other Countries Educate Their Children*. Lancaster, Pa.: Technomic, 1993.

McDonagh, W. "Travellers and the Issue of Education: A Parent's Perspective." *Glocklai* 2 (November 1997): 18-19.

National Commission on Excellence in Education. *A Nation at Risk: The Imperative for Educational Reform.* Washington, D.C.: U.S. Government Printing Office, 1983.

National Council for Curriculum and Assessment (NCAA). *Curriculum for Primary Schools: Language.* Dublin, 1997.

National Council for Curriculum and Assessment (NCAA). *Primary School Curriculum.* Dublin, 1999.

National Curriculum Council. *Starting Out with the National Curriculum: An Introduction to the National Curriculum and Religious Education.* York, U.K., 1992.

Ni Chleirigh, I. "Comparative Studies of L2 and L3 Learners in the Primary School." Master's thesis, Trinity College, Dublin, 1990.

O'Brien, A. "Second Level Education for Traveller Children: A Case Study." *Glocklai* 2 (November 1997): 22-24.

Office for Standards in Education (OFSTED). *School-Centered Initial Teacher Training: 1993-1994.* London: Her Majesty's Stationery Office, 1995.

Office of Population Censuses and Surveys (OPCS). *1991 Census: Preliminary Report for England and Wales.* London: Her Majesty's Stationery Office, 1991.

Office of Population Censuses and Surveys (OPCS). *Labor Force Survey 1990 and 1991.* London: Her Majesty's Stationery Office, 1992. a

Office of Population Censuses and Surveys (OPCS). *1991 Census Definitions: Great Britain.* London: Her Majesty's Stationery Office, 1992. b

Office of Population Censuses and Surveys (OPCS). *1991 Census: Sex, Age, Marital Status.* London: Her Majesty's Stationery Office, 1993. a

Office of Population Censuses and Surveys (OPCS). *1991 Census report for Great Britain (Part I), vol. I.* London: Her Majesty's Stationery Office, 1993. b

Osborne, R.D. "Education in Northern Ireland." In *After the Reforms: Education and Policy in Northern Ireland,* edited by R.D. Osborne et al. Aldershot, U.K.: Avebury, 1993.

Pollard, A. *An Introduction to Primary Education: For Parents, Governors, and Student Teachers.* London: Cassell, 1996.

Raffe, D. "Upper Secondary Education." In *Education in Scotland: Policy and Practice from Pre-School to Secondary,* edited by M.M. Clark and P. Munn. London: Routledge, 1997.

Ranger, C. *Ethnic Minority Teachers*. London: Commission for Racial Equality, 1988.

Ross, H.; Cave, W.; and Blair, D.E. "On Shifting Ground: The Post-Paradigm Identity of American Comparative Education, 1979-1988." *Compare* 22, no. 2 (1992): 113-31.

"Save the Teacher." *Sunday Times*, 31 May 1998, pp. 5, 3.

Scottish Consultative Council on the Curriculum (SCCC). *Teaching for Effective Learning*. Dundee, 1996.

Scottish Education Department. *The Structure of the Curriculum in the Third and Fourth Years of the Scottish Secondary School*. Edinburgh: Her Majesty's Stationery Office, 1997.

Scottish Office Education Department (SOED). *Upper Secondary Education in Scotland: Report of the Committee to Review Curriculum and Examinations in the Fifth and Sixth Years of Secondary Education in Scotland* (the Howie Report). Edinburgh: Her Majesty's Stationary Office, 1992.

Scottish Office Education and Industry Department (SOEID). *The Structure and Balance of the Curriculum 5-14*. Edinburgh: Her Majesty's Stationery Office, 1993.

Scottish Office Education and Industry Department. *Higher Still: Opportunity for All*. Edinburgh: Her Majesty's Stationery Office, 1994.

Scottish Office Education and Industry Department (SOEID). *Scottish Education Statistics: 1996 Edition 1*. Edinburgh: Her Majesty's Stationery Office, 1996. a

Scottish Office Education and Industry Department (SOEID). *Memorandum on Early Entrance Requirements to Courses of Teacher Education in Scotland*. Edinburgh: Her Majesty's Stationery Office, 1996. b

Walford, G. *Life in Public Schools*. London: Methuen, 1986.

ABOUT THE AUTHOR

James E. Green is a professor of Educational Administration at California State University, San Bernardino. Prior to his career in higher education he was a teacher and administrator in public schools. He is author or co-author of numerous publications, including two PDK fastbacks — *Tech Prep: A Strategy for School Reform* and *State Academies for the Academically Gifted*. For the past eight years he has been a lecturer with PDK's Author Lecture Series. Green began his research for *Education in the United Kingdom and Ireland* while residing at Wroxton College in England during the summer, 1996.